WORTH IT

&

WONDERFUL

CAITLYN SCAGGS

WORTH IT
&
WONDERFUL

INSPIRATION FOR CHRISTIAN WOMEN
TO LIVE BRAVELY AND BOLDLY

Morehouse Publishing
NEW YORK

Morehouse Publishing, 19 East 34th Street, New York, NY 10016

Morehouse Publishing is an imprint of Church Publishing Incorporated.

Cover design by Paul Soupiset

A record of this book is available from the Library of Congress.

ISBN 978-1-64065-602-4 (hardcover)
ISBN 978-1-64065-603-1 (ebook)

This book is dedicated to the Scaggs Squad:
Adam, Harper, and Peyton.
The more I know you, the more I love you.

CONTENTS

ACKNOWLEDGMENTS

I'm writing these acknowledgments with a huge smile on my face. I love people, and this portion of my book is a beautiful celebration of those who have poured into me and my dream.

To my husband, Adam: Thank you for being a strong and steady source of support across all of life's many adventures. A lot has changed since we said, "I do," but I'm thankful that our love and commitment have remained the same, regardless of the twists and turns of life.

To Harper and Peyton: I will always celebrate who God made you to be and that He handpicked me to be your mom. I don't just love you—I genuinely enjoy who you are. "If you need me, you know where I'll be … I'll be riding shotgun!"

Thank you to my mom and dad! You raised me to believe my voice matters, and that is one of the most profound gifts you have given me. I've never doubted that you are proud of me—book or no book. Thank you for the many practical ways you supported this dream—from answering teary phone calls to editing numerous drafts of the project.

To my amazing siblings and siblings-in-law, I'm thankful for the supportive family unit that we are! I value our ability to laugh, cry, and live life alongside each other. Rose—my little flower—you are a cycle-breaking inspiration. Thank you, Hannah, for cheering loud and being an honest source of perspective (our walks are SO good for the soul!). Kate, I love that you are a co-creative and will enter into brave places of bold dreams. Caleb, you are simply the coolest and have a heart of gold I admire so much! Joshua, I love that you are a deep thinker and invite me to do the same.

Thanks to my dear friends Brian and Marisela, your friendship feels more like family at this point. You show up for me over and over. Brian, thank you for asking how the book was going—especially on the days that I thought it was going nowhere.

To Samantha, you cheer the loudest and are the first to celebrate the success of others. Thank you for that gift of endless encouragement both professionally and personally—#obviously. Jennifer, thank you for helping me grow in leadership all those years ago. I carry so much of your insight with me, to this day. Eric, thanks for being the first person to suggest I should write a book—back in the day when I was still a police officer.

My heartfelt thanks to the team at Inspiration Ministries for allowing me to contribute to Kingdom Impact through written contributions. Craig, I appreciate that you were the first to welcome my writing and offer support. Michael and John, it has been a joy to work alongside you with a goal of spreading the Good News far and wide.

To my WDBJ7 friends, I've loved each episode of Mornin' Motivations and the opportunity to bring ideas within this book to life on camera. Kimberly, it's such a joy to work with you. Katey, thank you for getting us started and continuing to cheer from afar—including being an awesome editor.

To my literary agent, Linda Konner, I'm forever grateful that you took a chance on a debut author with a big dream for impact. Your patience and willingness to wait for the right time was exactly what was needed. I have valued your ideas and input as much as your confidence in the process.

My sincere thanks to Airié Stuart. God knew I needed you to be the editor! I have loved our many conversations and how real each interaction is. You have made me feel supported and valued as a "newbie" to the publishing world. Thank you for celebrating my voice and encouraging me to make sure it always shows up. I appreciate you and the entire Church Publishing team so very much.

To my New Hope Girls family, you are a living testimony to the power of our True Hope. You have shaped me as a woman of faith and had such a monumental impact on this book. Wanda, you are a fierce woman of faith and someone I admire deeply—a beautiful warrior. Joy, I value being your sister-in-Christ so much. Thank you for pointing me to scripture and truth, while also being an incredibly fun friend!

Every person I have mentioned is a direct blessing from above! I recognize that God provided me with the right people, at the right time, to bring this book to fruition. He is able to do immeasurably more than I could have ever hoped or dreamed—and that is the most important acknowledgment of all. *To live is Christ*, and I'm thankful for the ability I have to live boldly and bravely for Him.

CHAPTER 1

INTRODUCTION

I know we aren't supposed to worry—but I'm sitting here worried about you.

What exactly has me worried about you? Well, if you must know ...

I'm concerned you don't realize just how wonderful you are. I'm afraid you may not understand the depths of your value—of your worthiness.

My swirling concern relates to what I've observed in so many women. I see women who don't fully grasp their value and as a result are living life with a fraction of the abundance they could be experiencing. Rather than living vibrant lives that are marked by possibilities, they allow themselves to be oversimplified and relegated to cautious and subdued living.

I wonder if you are holding parts of yourself back and failing to pursue your dreams? Are you living with cloaked insecurities and fear of the future? Can you honestly say that you greet each day with your most wholehearted and authentic self?

The Bible consistently affirms just how valuable you are. Scripture also makes it clear that as you journey through life you are intended to be transformed as you go.[1] It's not about being who everyone else thinks you should be or taking the pre-prescribed path the world expects you to follow. No, this is about you welcoming who you are and who God lovingly made you to be.

I hope to encourage you into a place of soul-satisfying living, based on the belief that what God says about you is true. I invite you to embrace every one of the complex, nuanced, and intricate realities of who you are. Together, we will commit to living brave and bold lives. We will go on a journey of self-discovery, reflection, and biblical empowerment. We will unpack what it means to step into an identity that is defined by who God says you are—not who the world says you should be.

I hope this will be eye-opening and that you will be set free from the traps of not feeling smart enough, pretty enough, or accomplished enough. You will learn practical steps for how to release thoughts that tell you you're not a good enough mom or successful enough career woman. You will be encouraged to fight unkind self-talk, impostor syndrome, and narratives that don't serve you well.

It's time to explore how you can be released from the ugly lies and unfair expectations that are causing your brilliance and shine to be dimmed by guilt, frustration, and shame. Rooted in new perspective for your life, you will reframe how you see yourself and approach the world.

This book was written to beckon you into the beautiful reality that God says you are enough—He says you are worth it and wonderful.

---

1. 2 Corinthians 3:18

It's my sincere hope that, armed with a new-found belief that you matter deeply, you will be

> God says you are enough—He says you are worth it and wonderful.

able to push through the exhaustion and demands of everyday life and into a place of dynamic living. I hope to inspire you to embrace the life you've been given! To lean into the unique and wonderful creation that you are, while making the maximum impact on this world.

This book is a shared battle cry for us to fully own all we are and all the potential we embody. It matters that we have a strategy to guide us, a plan to propel us forward, and a clear vision for what victory can and will look like. This includes embracing the challenges we will undoubtedly face.

I'm not here to pretend that the world is always sunny, and the days are all good. But I will still challenge you to live bravely and boldly regardless of what comes your way. You only get one shot at this thing called life—make it a joyful, abundant, and colorful story you are proud to tell.

Are you ready? It's time to live like you are worth it and wonderful—because you are!

I'm so glad you are joining me on this journey! At the end of each chapter, I will provide you a guided way to reflect on the chapter and apply the concepts to your life. Before you continue, can we connect on social media? Keep me posted as your brave and bold journey unfolds!

@CaitlynScaggs

"Boldly Pursue with Caitlyn Scaggs"

CHAPTER 2

IT'S TIME TO BE BRAVE AND BOLD

How did you get here? How would you describe your journey to this exact place and time?

One of my favorite aspects of getting to know people is learning about how their story has evolved in both expected and unexpected ways. I'm so curious about the twists and turns that have informed who you have become over the course of your life. Think about them and consider what some of your major milestone moments have been.

As I reflect on my own path, I realize that my commitment to embracing self-ownership and personal complexities is largely due to the variety of distinct roles I have taken on over my lifetime. Brace yourself, there have been many!

I'm a wife, a mother, a friend, but I've also been a police officer, an entrepreneur, and a business leader across different industries. I regularly appear on the news and work for a non-profit that helps fight human trafficking. There has been so much change running through the narrative of my life that

I have periodically wondered—am I really the same person who went to the police academy all those years ago?

I wonder if you ever feel the same way—like life has gone in such unexpected directions that you have to squint and stare really hard in the mirror to even recognize yourself anymore? Finding myself in that position (more than once) has made me think hard—really hard—about what has been consistent across all of those seasons and roles. Reflecting on the twists and turns, ups and downs, and joys and hardships of my journey has resulted in clarity about what exactly has led me to a place of authentic living.

Would you like to know what my big "Ah-ha" has been?

It's the wonderful truth that I get to be who God made me to be, not who the world says I am! That may sound overly simple, but let me invite you into the light bulb moment that made it all so clear!

I'm a bookworm so it's no surprise to me that reading helped flip the switch! In the iconic business book, "Built to Last" by Jim Collins and Jerry Porras,[1] the authors share their extensive study of companies that have been wildly successful across time. Those winning companies were then contrasted with others from the same industry that were good but not great. The core differentiating factors were shared, discussed, and explored.

One of the factors they uncovered, that helped the great rise above the good, was rejecting the "tyranny of the or" and embracing the "genius of the and." An example of this is a business that embraces both low-price and high-quality products; they don't choose one or the other. At the time I

---

1. Collins, J. C., & Porras, J. I. (1997). Built to last: Successful habits of visionary companies. New York: HarperBusiness.

read these words I was an entrepreneur who was nurturing my startup marketing agency. The concept felt important as I dreamed about what the future of our company would look like. But I also realized Collins and Porras were on to something that applies not just to successful corporations but also to each of us as individuals.

There is genius in your personal "ands"—when you can embrace realities that others might argue are opposite and exclusive qualities. For example, there is power in your ability to be both lovely and fierce at the same time. You don't need to feel compelled to be one or the other, which would be the "tyranny of the or." It's possible for you to lean into both.

It isn't just these iconic business leaders who are suggesting you should reject limiting exclusivities. The Bible itself is full of paradox and contrast that are used to illustrate the transformative power of a life deeply rooted in God's truth.

The first shall be last and the last shall be first.
—Matthew 20:16

In our weakness we are made strong.
—2 Corinthians 12:10

The light shines in the darkness.
—John 1:5

Live in the world but not of the world.
—John 17:14–18

The old is made new.
—2 Corinthians 5:17

Beauty for ashes.
—Isaiah 61:3

Having nothing, yet possessing everything.
—2 Corinthians 6:10b

It's clear that contrast and complexities are woven throughout scripture as a means of affirming our innate value, underscoring God's deep love for us, and helping us better understand who we were made to be. The powerful paradoxes found throughout scripture affirm that we were created for a life of purpose.

> The powerful paradoxes found throughout scripture affirm that we were created for a life of purpose.

And yet, it seems that women largely live feeling pressure to simplify themselves. We experience too many choices that are stark in contrast, one or the other, either/or. In response to this forced decision-making, we inevitably wrestle with wanting to have it all. Then we can feel guilt and shame for wanting to have it all. We pursue all the things the world tells us we should, then we enter a place of feeling burnt out, overworked, and underutilized. Our days may feel devoid of joy and in our hearts we remain hungry.

I wonder if instead of choosing what feels true to who you are, you instead choose what the world tells you that you should choose. Or do you feel guilty because deep within yourself you sense that God has more for you and you know you aren't pursuing it?

It could be that you are choosing between what you perceive to be mutually exclusive options. Could it be that you are settling? Are you allowing your decisions to be made by pressure instead of your purpose? You can't forget that God promises He has more in mind for you than you could ever imagine.[2]

---

2. Ephesians 3:20

With that realization in mind, I suggest you ask yourself why you would spend your time on Earth settling for a mediocre and "going through the motions" type of living when you could instead choose vibrant and purpose-driven living.

A key to pursuing an outstanding life marked by lasting impact is rooting your identity in God's definition of who you are, rather than a worldly definition of who you are. This will propel you forward with purpose and joy. Living authentically with faith as your compass enables you to leave the maximum impact.

Crushing Contrast

Just as Porras and Collins identified the tyranny of the or as a threat to exceptional businesses, I've noticed that crushing contrast is a threat to exceptional living.

People like clearly-defined categories because it creates order for how we experience the world. It helps make sense of the flood of information we process each and every day, from the weather to marketing messages and our schedules for the day. That's just barely scratching the surface! Think about all the Instagram posts, Facebook messages, emails, and texts you are also reading and considering as your day unfolds. Your brain needs to simplify somewhere, and categories are a way to do exactly that. It makes sense.

Often, clearly defined categories and simplification aren't such a bad thing. On the surface, they appear to make life easier. Are you a coffee or tea kind of girl? Morning or night person? Do you like vacations in the mountains or by the ocean? All of those categories are totally innocuous and a fun way to boil you down to an either/or existence. However, when the oversimplification is regarding the core of who you are, and who God made you to be it becomes a problem, a big problem.

There is a good chance you are complicit in your own categorization and oversimplification. This can happen without you even being consciously aware of what you are doing. After all, opposites and contrast are a core part of our reality from the earliest days of education. Before you even started kindergarten, I imagine you were learning about opposites: up or down, happy or sad, big or small. As you aged and matured, the opposites grew in complexity and in implication: family or career, responsible or joyful, strategic or spontaneous.

These qualities are often regarded as impossible to coexist within one person. But guess what? You are a beautiful, complex, and dynamic masterpiece. You can occupy seemingly opposite attributes and embrace the outcomes of joy, meaning and depth that emerge. In doing so, your authentic and honest-to-goodness self will emerge.

> You are a beautiful, complex, and dynamic masterpiece.

It may seem that society and culture want you to choose between invisible yet powerful forces. But why pick sides? Why not pick all of it? It's worth embracing complexities and rejecting oversimplified categories. When you allow yourself to be both, to occupy the opposites, you can shift your focus to the truth about who you are and all that you were created to be—by God Himself. Doesn't it make sense that you would trust your Creator to explain who you are—rather than your co-creation?

I'm not suggesting that you compromise between two ends of the spectrum. Rather, I'm saying that you can choose to be fully family-focused and career-driven. You can choose to be responsible and joyful, independent and supported by others, lovely and fierce. When it comes to the qualities we embody, you can be it all.

Choosing to embrace our complexities and this type of paradoxical living takes perseverance, persistence, and a strong backbone. It's up to you to battle for the vibrant life you were created to live. It's up to you to own and embrace the wonderful complexities of who God made you to be. Remember, you are a masterpiece!

> It's up to you to own and embrace the wonderful complexities of who God made you to be. Remember, you are a masterpiece!

I personally love Psalm 139:14, a verse written by King David, "Thank you for making me so wonderfully complex! Your workmanship is marvelous—how well I know it."[3] Are you smiling right now? I am! The Bible affirms how wonderfully complex we each are. It's in the black and white text that we are marvelous—that you are marvelous. How's that for some encouraging and powerful truth?

Yet, I see so many women who have not let this truth wash over them and impact their everyday living, and this breaks my heart. When thinking about the pressure to pick between opposites, and live in an oversimplified way, I find it to be a harsh expectation. The contrast becomes crushing when we feel forced to choose. I have met many women who feel inadequate, not enough, and just not right. It's a tiring and weary

---

3. Psalm 139:14 (NLT)

state of being. It's a broken record of discouragement. It's not the joyful life that we are invited into by God Himself.

This begs the question as to why we do this to ourselves? Why do we succumb to patterns and expectations that reduce us to an oversimplified shadow of the brilliance we were made to embody? I believe that in part it's because of how much easier it is to keep things simple! When things get more complicated, well, they are more complicated!

It's easier to say, "She's a real career woman!" It's more cumbersome to say, "She's really dedicated to her career, but, wow, she has such a great family life too!" Assuming that she really is a woman who embraces both her career and her family, isn't it a more generous and truthful description to describe her in that way? Doesn't it paint a more holistic picture? Yes, but it also requires more qualifying, additional words and additional intention. But it's worth it because she's worth it.

It's time to insist the rules and mindsets change! You must be comfortable challenging deeply rooted behavior patterns and age-old narratives. Armed with your faith and rooted in God's truth, this becomes possible. Prepare yourself to put in the work required to think differently and introspectively. Consider the fundamental faith foundation you know to be true and whether you are aligning that truth with your self-assessment and worth. It matters that you step into all that you are and all you were made to be. It matters that you live a life of vibrancy.

> Consider the fundamental faith foundation you know to be true and whether you are aligning that truth with your self-assessment and worth.

As you allow yourself to consider how you are worth it and wonderful, you will enjoy a journey of self-discovery and biblical empowerment that is fruitful in depth, joy, and meaning.

While you turn the pages of this book you are going to spend time exploring the paradoxes many of us face over the course of our lifetime, the opposites that compete for who we are and threaten to steal our abundance. These mutually exclusive options leave you not just feeling pulled in multiple directions but truly pulled apart.

You will also learn to identify the characteristics needed to pursue a life that is lived fully and rooted in faith convictions. It isn't easy and it doesn't happen overnight. It also isn't something that is one-and-done. It takes care, commitment, growth, and refinement to live a life marked by this kind of abundance.

Abundance isn't about what you can hold in your hand. It's not financial prosperity or a smooth-sailing life. It's wonder, awe, gratitude and soul-satisfaction rolled up into one amazing feeling. An abundant life is a truly empowered life.

> An abundant life is a truly empowered life.

You have an opportunity to embrace your complexities instead of being crushed by contrast.

You can be strategic and spontaneous.

You can be broken and whole.

You can be career focused and family focused.

You can be responsible and joyful.

You can be lovely and fierce.

You can be confident and humble.

You can be independent and supported.

You can be ambitious and content.

You can be adventurous and wise.

You can live a life that reflects the beautiful reality that you are wonderful and worth it.

Ultimately, you can boldly pursue boundless living rooted in the truth of who you are and whose you are because of who Jesus is and what He has done. He is our ultimate hope and the reason we can live bold and brave lives that shine bright[4].

Emboldened by Faith

Sometimes people I know describe me as brave and bold and every time it makes me laugh a bit nervously. That feedback makes me squirm a little bit because I'm so aware of the insecurities, doubts, and anxieties I fight. I know I'm not unique in carrying the weight of self-doubt. You might know what I mean?

However, when I take a step back and consider what others are seeing I can only attribute it to how I am emboldened by my faith.

Faith is an interesting word. It can mean something different to each person. I do think it can be used in a semi-secular sense to signal an optimistic belief that everything will work out just fine. I also think the word can nod to a generalized belief in some higher power who is at work and configuring circumstances and situations on our behalf. I'm not talking about either definition when I use the word.

My faith is in a living God who is engaged with humanity. I'm certain that I can trust Him no matter what and that what He says within the pages of the Bible is true. In the

---

4. John 12:46

nooks and crannies of my soul there is a transformative truth that has found a home. The truth is that God loves me abundantly and because of that I can feel unshakable confidence in my worth and the possibilities for my life. It's not because I'm great that I can be bold, it's because of God's greatness.

> It's not because I'm great that I can be bold, it's because of God's greatness.

Growing up in a loving and Christian home provided me with a faith foundation and I was blessed with two incredible parents who guided me as I grew. I watched what their faith meant to them and learned so much in those formative years. However, there came a day where I had to claim my faith personally and on my own two feet. I realized that I could not rely on other people to choose for me. I had to nurture and grow the seeds that had been planted.

Even if you have been a faithful person your whole life, you may need to grab onto your faith in a new way. It's a beautiful kind of empowerment when you realize your faith can be fully your own! You can pursue and determine where you will anchor you own life and what compass will guide you along your journey.

For me, the bold quality of my faith emerged when I was a police officer. I began that job fresh out of college and full of idealistic views of how I would change the world. I quickly became appalled at how sad, devastating, and heavy the world can be. I found myself staring at the brokenness of the world on each of my patrol shifts.

You might ask, what did I expect when I signed up for law enforcement? Great question! I dreamed of being a cop because I wanted to positively impact others, but, in reality, I found each shift was a new opportunity to be disappointed.

Life can be like that sometimes, can't it? Disappointing and completely out of alignment with what we expect. There are Instagram-perfect snapshots in our mind of what it will all look like and then we are hit with an ugly reality that leaves us reeling. In one way or another, at one time or another, we all are faced with that harsh reality of disappointment and disillusionment.

My nights on midnight shift were riddled with mental health crises, domestic violence, abuse of children, and devastating car accidents. Each shift was a fresh opportunity to deal with heartache, pain, brokenness, and people at their very worst. There are still calls I can't unsee or forget. The man beaten within inches of his life who will never come out a vegetative state. The teenage girl who took her life—and how her mom couldn't stop screaming. The domestic violence call where the little girl was so afraid, she wet herself. Night after night, I was reminded of the tragedies of human life. I got to the point where I wondered who I was really helping. In my most honest moments I would have dejectedly whispered: nobody.

Does your story include moments marked by hopelessness? It doesn't take wearing a bulletproof vest and badge to encounter despair and darkness. It could be a profound personal disappointment you still carry. Or your community could have experienced major tragedy that left behind deep scars. It also could be feelings of overwhelm as you consume headlines that remind you just how sad this world can be. If hopelessness has been a part of your story—or is a reality you are living—I hope you will hold on. Let's keep exploring this together. Hopelessness doesn't need to be the conclusion; it wasn't for me, and I don't want it to be for you either.

> Hopelessness doesn't need to be the conclusion; it wasn't for me, and I don't want it to be for you either.

My battle with hopelessness continued for a couple of years. It got to the point where I realized the brokenness I witnessed was encroaching on my heart and spirit. It was nothing that anyone else could see. Life was generally bumping along just fine on the outside. But inside, a plague was destroying my joy and ravaging my heart. A dark cloud of cynicism was lingering, invisible to the outside world but tangible to me.

There came a day when I when I had a stark realization about what was going on within me. It was a very specific day with a specific situation and a specific moment. I can still see it all and feel it all. I was the first officer on scene at a suicide attempt. The man was in excruciating emotional pain and from that deep place of brokenness he began shrieking extensive profanities at me and then at God. There was blood, tears and rage. He poured out fury from his most deep core.

It frightened me far more than any domestic disturbance or fight call I had responded to. It was terrifying because it underscored that the battles I was experiencing at work were not of the flesh and blood but were spiritual in nature.[5] That was my tipping point for a choosing a life marked by faith and a personal relationship with God. I knew I desperately needed Him if I had any hope of emotionally surviving my job as a police officer. However, more than that, I knew I

5. Ephesians 6:12

needed faith in order to live each day abundantly in a world ravaged by heartbreak.

I began listening to our church's podcasts each morning when I got off work and went for a run. At that time, our pastor was in an extended series in the chapter of Luke. It was perfect timing and exactly what I needed to hear!

Luke is a fantastic account of the many ways that Jesus served and loved. He met people in the darkest of circumstances, who were facing a variety of hardships, and ushered in healing, love and redemption. From prostitutes to lepers, the lame to societal castaways, Jesus looked people in the eyes and wasn't afraid of their messes. As my pastor navigated these passages of scripture, he kept reminding us that there is always hope because of Jesus. We can get our hopes up!

Have you found yourself looking heavenward and asking, "Why?!" Have you experienced hardship that has hardened your heart? I want to encourage you to grab onto hope with both hands. Yes, it can be so hard. I will admit that I struggled to initially believe hope could take root in my heart. Not with the darkness and destruction I was enmeshed in at work. How can there be hope in devastating mental health struggles? How is there hope when an 18-month-old has broken bones and a bruised body from abuse? How is there hope when a car accident kills a mother and son who were simply on their way home from the store? How is there hope?

And yet, the more I learned the more I wanted to believe. My soul craved the transformational truth I was discovering. I felt beckoned to the beauty of the Gospel. The more I heard the more I felt it could be true and it had to be true. I believed.

I decided to get my hopes up in Jesus. And that changed everything.

I began approaching each shift with a different perspective—one that was faith-based. I prayed throughout the nights for my fellow officers and the people I encountered on my calls. On my dinner breaks I would take my Bible out and reflect on truth and things from above. I listened to sermons and podcasts while I was cruising around. Soon, my heart was able to handle the tough stuff because I knew that my hope was no longer in my badge. Through the challenges of law enforcement, I found new understandings of the impact of faith.

I sincerely hope you have been able to slip into a sweet place of blessed assurance that God is for you and a love relationship with Jesus changes everything. However, if you are wrestling with this reality and exploring your faith as we speak, it's okay. Take a deep breath and allow yourself to be open to faith-possibilities. Don't add any pressure or feel the need to force the issue. God is invitational and relentless in His pursuit of each of us. I urge you to be open to where your journey may go next.

After wrestling with my faith, I realized that God wants me to invite Him into the broken, bruised, and painful places that don't make sense. All the while, I feel His reassuring words of truth over me.

I am His.

I am seen.

I am beloved.

I can trust Him no matter what.

I am a daughter of the Most High.

I am loved with a sacrificial, all encompassing, boundless love.

He restores what was once lost.

He will provide.

He is my living hope.

Tell me this: If the God of the Universe feels this way about me, then who am I not to step into my purpose? Why would I let the broken systems of the world define who I should be when God's word is so clear about my identity?

When I allowed my identity to be defined by these truths, I became brave and bold.

My ability to be brave is because my confidence is in something so much more than myself. My faith impacts my dreams, my conversations, the workplace, my marriage, my parenting, our home, the places we go and the people I see. The abundant love of God yields abundance in my life.

Are You Brave?

Is your life marked by bravery? Are you living as if the world needs you and the gifts you have to give? Are you showing up as your honest, authentic self to contribute and shine bright?

Maybe your honest answer is yes! If so, I love that. Keep living brave because goodness knows, we need you! You are shining a beautiful light for others and inviting them to do the same.

Maybe your honest answer is no. If so, I love that too. When we can be honest with each other and ourselves there is room for growth and if necessary, healing. I sincerely hope this is a moment where you start to consider the powerful possibilities of brave living.

Living with an identity rooted in who God says you are truly takes courage! It means pushing back on cultural currents that want you to play it safe and live small. As you push back and swim upstream you must get comfortable with the work, effort, and attention that it takes. At times, you must also enter places of discomfort and tension as you feel the contrasting priorities vying for your time and attention.

As you pursue brave living you may realize that the future looks a bit fuzzy or unclear. It's so hard to feel a stirring and a yearning but not be able to fully see the path forward. It's in those moments that our actionable faith has to drive us ahead with confidence in God's leadership over our lives.

I have learned to be content with one step at a time, even if those steps feel unsteady. I may not always be entirely sure where the path is leading, but I know I'm moving toward God's best for me. Lingering in the fog of uncertainty, however uncomfortable, means I will emerge on the other side and experience delight. So I press on.

I feel it right now as I write these words. My kids are downstairs watching a cartoon before bed. My husband is working on a jigsaw puzzle. I just finished cleaning the dishes, tidying up the house and working on my grad school homework. The day has taken so much from me. I'm exhausted. Yet, I feel this nagging tension to get my thoughts, ideas, and dreams out into the atmosphere.

Writing this book has been a desire God placed in my heart. Even though many times I wanted to give up on the dream (and believe me, I tried!). God kept urging me forward, prompting me to be brave with my life. Leaning into my faith gives me the courage to keep pushing, even when things feel hard. Faith makes me courageous, and I know it can do the same for you.

Are You Bold?

Are you bold in your belief that you matter? Have you had your moment in which truth washes over you in a way that changes everything? If not, I encourage you to be very curious as you read through the pages to come. Look for how Jesus shows up to impact even the most seemingly benign and mundane areas of my life. He can do the same for you! Consider what it could mean for you to allow yourself to be transformed at a soul-level. Invite faith into your everyday experiences and especially into your self-concept.

Let's be clear. Being bold isn't about being over-the-top or obnoxious. Some like to mistakenly swap the word bold for "rude" or "presumptuous." That's not the definition I'm using. Being bold is living with enthusiasm and an intention to squeeze every bit of goodness out of life because you are confident that it's what God intends for you.

It's quite clear within the pages of scripture that you are intended to live a

> Being bold is living with enthusiasm and an intention to squeeze every bit of goodness out of life because you are confident that it's what God intends for you.

beautiful life. Not a perfect life. Not a life without hardship. But a life marked by joy regardless of your circumstances.[6] That is the boldest type of living, living in a way that rises

---

6. 1 Thessalonians 5:16–18

above the tough stuff in this world and shines bright all the while.

Easier said than done, right? The Bible tells us that there is a battle raging that threatens to thwart our abundance. John 10:10 tells us, "The thief comes only to steal and kill and destroy. I came that they may have life and have it abundantly." Come what may, you are meant to live abundantly.

We Need You

For just a moment I want to make this not about you and rather about us. We need you.

The world needs more people who reflect true hope to a hurting world. We need you to be your best, most brave, and most bold self.

> The world needs more people who reflect true hope to a hurting world.

When you are empowered by faith, you will serve others, change the game, leave a lasting impact and challenge the status quo in all the right ways. This type of living will encourage opportunity and leave the promise of possibility in your wake. Be a radiant light! We need you to show up as the wonderfully complex person you were made to be.

It's time you reject the idea that you must quietly comply with oversimplified expectations. It's time you purposely step into who you are. It's time to live bravely and boldly—so how about it, are you in? Are you willing to honestly explore what that can look like?

My goal is to urge YOU forward, toward God's best, while constantly reminding you to seek your identity in Him first. That is what inspired me to share my story and authentically reflect on the lessons I've learned along this beautiful, bumpy, and meaningful journey. This is for you.

Brave and Bold Steps Forward

Living into the reality that you are worth it and wonderful requires commitment and work! Take time to reflect on the questions below before diving into the rest of the book.

1. In what areas of your life are you bold?
2. How have insecurities and doubts held you back in the past?
3. Have you experienced a major "faith moment" on your journey? Write about exactly how it felt when it happened.
4. What is one God-given quality that you like about yourself?
5. As you prepare to dive into this book, what are you most eager for?

CHAPTER 3

STRATEGIC AND SPONTANEOUS

We all know that woman who can't go anywhere without her planner. Not a digital app but a bound book that houses her color-coded schedule. With her colorful pens and sticky tabs in hand she's always ready to update her schedule and plan for success.

We also all know that woman who thinks she's on time when she's only 5 minutes late. Can you think of who she is? Often, it's because something unexpected popped up at the last minute, from a long line at Starbucks to an empty gas tank.

Maybe we are one of those women! Do you love a perfect plan and enjoy strategically wrapping your hands around your schedule? Or maybe, you are a go-with-the flow kind of person and feel most alive when spontaneity drives your days.

I tend to lean heavily toward loving a well-crafted plan, although I don't have a perfectly color-coded planner to prove it. When it comes to making my plans, I'm often uncompromisingly stubborn and strategic. At my core, I tend to be a control freak. There, I said it.

My tendency to launch a well-crafted plan, with the goal of controlling and curating my life, was most evident on the early side of my career. "Back in the day" I was headstrong and certain that my destiny was in my hands. Toward the end of high school, and through most of college, I lacked a robust and engaged faith. My lack of faith is now obvious when I reflect on how much energy I expended trying to make my life exactly what I thought it should be.

Now I'm in a much different place where I will put a strategic plan into motion, but I also know it's important to go with the flow and leave some space for spontaneity. I fight being so meticulous that I'm planning past the blessings of today, failing to see all that God is providing and allowing for that guidance each step of the way. I've realized my determination needs to be matched with flexibility to allow divine interruptions in my days.

> I've realized my determination needs to be matched with flexibility to allow divine interruptions in my days.

Although usually a great quality, strategy in some situations can be to your detriment. It's possible to be so stubborn and controlling that you invite misery into your life. The misery can come from stress, anxiety and frustration or it can hurt relationships and cause strained connections. It also appears when you are so committed to one outcome that you fail to see other possibilities. Misery appears anytime you try to be your own god—failing to submit your life to your One True God.

You can also be flexible—or spontaneous—to a fault. Although spontaneous people are often seen as the fun one within a friend group or family, the lack of structure and planning can leave others frustrated. Colleagues may be annoyed and describe you as a flake. Rapidly changing plans or unexpected left turns can leave people dizzy in your wake. Failing to follow through may lead to wasted time and resources. You can also enter into places of misery when you fail to recognize your role in follow-through and "making it happen." After all, God asks you to show up and work hard, as if we are working for Him, not for people.[1]

Your ability to live a life marked by both strategy and spontaneity helps you move through your days with a loving dependence on the Lord. It creates an opportunity for you to listen well as you honor Him. Boldly embracing these seemingly opposite qualities is recognition that faith is the ultimate source of direction and rhythm in your life.

Does it sound complicated? It may sound that way, but I assure you this beautiful truth is something you can rest easy in. Honoring who God made you to be, and allowing faith to lead your every step, will always be worth it.

Strategically Stubborn

I've changed a lot over the last 20 years! If you had met me as I was transitioning from high school to college, you would have found someone exhaustingly obsessed with perfect plans. I was certain that I had the work ethic, intelligence, and endurance to accomplish any goal I set for myself. I

1. Colossians 3:23

didn't care how wild and outlandish it may have seemed to others. I deeply believed my parents when they said, "You can be anything you want to be when you grow up."

Looking back (while rolling my eyes) I can think of an analogy that helps bring to life my mindset. I'm reminded of the stubborn and slightly reckless attitude of a toddler. An attitude that is immature and a bit foolish. Toddlers may climb up a couch, perch themselves on top, and yell "watch this!" as they hurl themselves down—ever confident it will all go exactly as planned. Sometimes it works out fine. Sometimes it ends in a puddle of tears and with copious amounts of ice for the boo-boo. All the while, the parents are shaking their heads thinking, *"Wow, I saw that disaster coming. If only she had listened …"*

As a late-teen, I was certain I could strategically design my life. Not too unlike a toddler, I was hurling myself into all the things I thought mattered and would ensure a lifelong, stable and successful career. Instead of leaving space for spontaneity and enjoying the moments, I was near obsessed with career perfection. I wanted to show everyone all that I was capable of. My actions screamed, "watch this!" as I hurled myself into the next achievement. I moved ahead stubborn and sure, without letting God be part of my plans. All while I'm sure God was watching and wishing I would yield to His guidance and quit seeking achievements absent of Him.

I loved planning to a fault. Planning and strategizing around my life were all about control. My control. At my core, that reflected a lack of faith. However, as my faith has grown, so has my ability to trust my days, weeks, years, and lifetime to God.

Remember, I worry about you. That's how this whole book began, with that confession. So let me ask you, who is in control of your life right now? I'm a bit worried about how you might answer the question. Are you a toddler on top of a couch, preparing for another boo-boo?

> So let me ask you, who is in control of your life right now?

Don't be. God's ways are so much more perfect and powerful than anything you can accomplish on your own. Yield to His authority in your life and trust Him above all else—to include your ability to curate the life of your dreams. In that release, you'll learn to create space to see God at work.

Perfectly Laid Plans

I had the perfect pedigree for someone who would have a long, satisfying, and successful career in Law Enforcement. My ambition began back in high school and I was certain it would be my forever-career. I recognized Law Enforcement as a calling—not a career.

From high school on, I took determined and logical steps in that direction. I attended college and earned a criminal justice degree with a perfect 4.0 GPA. I had a prestigious internship with the FBI in one of their behavioral analysis units. In addition to my work within their Crimes Against Children unit, I was able to take some classes at the FBI Academy with law enforcement from around the country and I participated in their "Power PT" physical training classes.

Peppered within all those academics and the internship was ample amounts of volunteer work at the local Women's

Resource Center. I answered a crisis hotline, volunteered within a Domestic Violence shelter, and also went to the hospital as an advocate for sexual assault victims. On top of that, I was a member of a Criminal Justice Fraternity and ultimately served as president of the organization. I was determined to do it all and be it all.

After graduation, my career continued forward, exactly as planned. When I applied for various police officer positions, I was a highly competitive candidate. It was the next step in my progression of career perfection. I graduated from college and moved right into law enforcement as a patrol officer with a permanent assignment on midnight shift. I share all these nitty gritty details because I want you to see how "in it to win it" I was within my career.

Sometimes in life we have a dream and vision then every piece falls neatly into place as we watch that vision come together before our very eyes. It would be so simple if that is how life bumped along. However, I've found that this type of "just as I planned it would go" living isn't a guarantee and for so many, it's not a reality. Interesting and memorable life experiences often happen in

> Interesting and memorable life experiences often happen in between all our well laid plans.

between all our well laid plans. Before too long, that was a lesson I came to understand in a deeply personal way.

The unraveling of my plans didn't happen instantly. It was a series of compounding events that came together with a grand crescendo. I met my wonderful husband and we got married. We struggled to get pregnant. We were blessed to get pregnant and then I battled a melanoma diagnosis during the pregnancy. Life was unfolding in parallel to my career and ultimately drew me out of law enforcement.

Even though I had previously struggled so badly as a rookie, I had found how to do my job in a faith-shaped way. I didn't leave law enforcement because I no longer wanted to be a police officer, it was that I wanted to be present for our family more.

Law enforcement regularly demands the job must be prioritized over family and I was unwilling to accept that reality. I didn't want to be working the midnight shift and unavailable when my little girl had a bad dream. I didn't want to be stuck in court instead of attending her first field trip. I didn't want to be patrolling the streets on the weekends when we could be off on a family adventure. It was very clear there was a seismic shift in my heart that could not be satisfied until I was out of the profession. The shift felt God-given and clear.

Although I can talk about it with clarity and it all make so much sense now, it was panic-inducing back then. I was not cool, calm, and collected. I could not imagine there would be many options for someone with a degree in criminal justice and a handful of years' experience as a patrol officer. I felt as if a significant period in my life was wasted and had become obsolete. I had to choose to bravely put one foot in front of the other, and trust God was leading me.

As I let faith guide me along the scenic route of my career, I learned that in God's economy, nothing is ever wasted. I have taken so many skills and lessons learned as a cop and applied them to the colorful and meaningful roles I've had since.

> In God's economy, nothing is ever wasted.

What about you? What type of shifts and twists have happened in your life? I'm wondering if you have fully maximized on all that you learned in one season and how it has helped you in the next. The learning doesn't always happen instantly, and it can be so hard to see clearly when we feel like we are at the epicenter of chaos. I hope you will spend time in reflection about how God has found ways to use every disparate piece of your life, even the pieces that may feel wasted in this moment.

You are constantly learning as you go and sometimes the learning happens in the most unexpected moments and when everything seems to have gone off the rails. I hope you will be stubborn in your resolve to soak up everything those moments can teach you! Things will go wrong, and plans will go sideways, but you can be insistent in learning as your journey unfolds. Those learnings are a gift you can carry into the next adventure, even if you aren't exactly sure what it will be or how it will all come together. God is so great about making sense of our confusion.[2]

> God is so great about making sense of our confusion.

Faithfully Release Outcomes

As my career story so painfully details, one of the biggest areas of struggle for me has been how I want to plan and strategize around situations and the need to release control. With a white-knuckled grip, I want to make it happen and get it done. I'm confident in my ability to out-work,

---

2. 1 Corinthians 14:33

out-perform, out-think any challenge. This confidence moves past a faith-shaped way of living and attempts to take over someone else's job—God's.

From what I observe, and the conversations I have, I'm certain that it's not just me. We are all struggling in our own way with being control-freaks in our own lives. We all want to reason, configure, back channel, and curate the life of our dreams—sometimes to our detriment. Hey, I get it! You read how obsessively stubborn I was about creating a career that was invincible. I left no opportunity on the table and thought I was leaving nothing to chance. And then life happened.

> We all want to reason, configure, back channel, and curate the life of our dreams—sometimes to our detriment.

With years of distance between me and my career panic I can see so much more clearly and the lessons I learned are so poignant. I have become certain that whether or not well-laid plans work out is not our prerogative if you have prayerfully done your best, listening and obeying to all that God has asked of you. It's time for you to release.

This begs the question: what do you need to release today? What are you gripping with white knuckles and trying to configure into perfection? Like me, you may be trying to control your career. However, it isn't just in our careers that this is an issue. As a parent, we can have hopes and plans for our children, but then we watch them exercise free will and come alive as their own unique person. That can be incredibly hard if you feel their outcomes depend solely on you!

Often our love for plans and achieving outcomes also reflects belief that our identity is somehow defined by the things we can accomplish on our to-do list. It's as if we think the ability of life to fall into place, work out according to our plans, or happen as expected is reflective of our worth. Let me be clear, your worth is not reflected in your ability to move through life as strategically planned. Your worth and identity are determined by God, setting you free to be all you are capable of being.

> Often our love for plans and achieving outcomes also reflects belief that our identity is somehow defined by the things we can accomplish on our to-do list.

It can be so hard when we are distracted by only what we see—the tangible things in front of us that make the best outcome appear so clear. But you need to "walk by faith, not by sight."[3] God knows your heart, your every movement, and your true motives! In this big vast universe, He is never too busy to pay attention to YOU.

While you take the next right step, whether a strategic or spontaneous one, you must hold onto the truth that you need to be "steadfast, immovable" and with the realization that when your efforts are in step with God, nothing you do will be in vain.[4] I had to learn this truth within my own life. While I may not have known what was waiting on the other side of my career in Law Enforcement, God was already up to something great! I have learned that in our waiting and wondering, He is always working.

---

3. 2 Corinthians 5:7
4. 1 Corinthians 15:58

Beyond the lingering self-doubt, my biggest worry was I traded in a career that felt more like a calling for an opportunity to draw a paycheck. I could not have been more wrong!

I left law enforcement and entered into a career adventure I never saw coming: marketing, communications, and public relations. I was able to use the skills and talents that made me a great police officer and I applied these skills to my new role. As a police officer I was praised for being an excellent report writer, highly empathetic, and a strong communicator. These skills are tremendously valuable in a marketing context.

Little by little, I came alive in the challenge and creativity of it all! I soon found myself thriving. My newfound confidence and passion weren't instant. It became possible over time. I had a lot of fun seeing my ideas and actions result in measurable business outcomes. It was deeply satisfying! I never thought I could enjoy a career more than law enforcement, but I was wrong. A career I never saw coming invited me into new places of growth, excitement, and impact.

Through my new line of work, I learned a powerful lesson about having a plan but being willing to adapt when prompted to do so. This was the pivot point in my life in which I realized the power in spontaneity. I realized that we can have strategy and a roadmap, but God ultimately sees the direction we are driving, and He may ask us to make an unexpected quick turn.

I'm so curious about the perfectly laid plans you have set for your own life! I wonder if you have also experienced a major moment where those plans fell through. This is where you must enter into the space in

> When you leave space for spontaneity and unexpected developments, you invite wonder and awe into your journey.

which you are focused and intentional with your days but don't try to overly control the way your life story plays out. When you leave space for spontaneity and unexpected developments, you invite wonder and awe into your journey.

A 16-Hour Road Trip

My husband and I do tend to be planners. We have vacation schedules set pretty far in advance. At this point I'm not sure we'd survive without our shared Google calendar. When we had really little kids, spontaneity was especially hard to come by. Every trip out of the house felt monumental and like a chore. Did we have the diaper bag, change of clothes, snacks, toys, books, sunscreen, favorite lovey—all the essentials! At times, the effort of vacation outweighed the relaxation we had been seeking. However, as we've all grown, we have found more flexibility.

It's not only in the area of your career and life goals that strategy and spontaneity will invite God's best. In your personal life you have the opportunity to have a flexible plan that creates space for God to show up and delight you.

Recently, I realized just how flexible our family has become when I agreed to a last minute 16-hour road trip with my kids—and without my husband. You read that right—16 hours! I'm even a bit shocked as I read these words.

The trip came about last minute because it was an opportunity to see my sister Rose, who lives in Alaska. My family lives in Virginia so there is a lot of geography between us! When I found out we'd get to see her and her family if we were willing to take this spontaneous road trip, I knew the answer needed to be "yes."

That same week, my husband had training for work, which meant he was unavailable, but the kids and I were extra available. We already had booked other vacations, so there was no budget for airfare. If we were going to make it happen, it was going to be in the car. Fortunately, we were able to travel with seasoned pros! We made the trek with my brother's family caravan-style up to our family's home in Bristol, Maine.

I felt a thrill of adventure as the kids and I prepared to conquer something we'd never done before—an extensive road trip. The semi-impulsive "yes" to adventure was the starting point—but there were 32 hours of driving that still had to be completed as we ventured there and back.

Funny, sometimes I say "yes" to spontaneity and then have buyer's remorse. I realize that in saying yes, I now have to actually go with the flow and experience many unknowns as plans evolve in unexpected ways. Does that make you nervous too? Even though I'm much more flexible than I was years ago, I still must put in intentional work to grow in this area. I hope you'll do the same! Don't let emotions rob you of opportunities for adventure and fun!

Once I took a deep breath, and talked to my sister-in-law extensively, I knew that if we wanted to build beautiful memories on the way, we needed to be highly intentional in our approach. It began in the weeks leading up to our trip.

My daughter developed a poster countdown that she kept taped to her bedroom door. Each day she would check a box, indicating we were one day closer to our big adventure. With each check mark, the anticipation and excitement built. We'd dream about our favorite things to do—from getting Penny Candy to ocean kayaking, visiting Monhegan Island to eating lobster on the docks. I wanted them to keep their eye on the finish line!

I also talked to them about how they could choose their attitude for the road trip. If they decided it was going to be long and miserable then I felt confident it would be! Conversely, if they were willing to believe it could be an adventure, it also could be that too. I made sure they realized they had an active role in deciding the outcome of our experience.

We all have people in our lives that are looking to us to determine how they should feel about a situation or experience. As you embrace strategy and spontaneity remember that others are watching! Children are especially observant and will often take on the emotions and attitudes of their parents. If not children, coworkers, or your friends. Consider how you are setting the tone for experiences and situations. Also remember that as you live bravely and boldly you encourage others to do the same!

I like to actively process out loud with my family so they see how I'm choosing a good attitude or actively working to create conditions for success. We all have eyes on us, learning from the way we live our lives, make sure you are proud of the lessons you are teaching.

> We all have eyes on us, learning from the way we live our lives, make sure you are proud of the lessons you are teaching.

In addition to packing our good attitudes, we had all sorts of practical solutions in place. Each kid had road trip necessities within arm's reach. Their door compartments had napkins, tissues, and hand sanitizer. I had a snack bag they could reach unassisted. We also had water bottles but discussed not drinking too much because each bathroom stop would make the trip take even longer. Within their backpacks they had lots of movie options for their personal DVD players, little action figures, and coloring books. I was ready with all the road trip supplies! I even remembered to give my car-sick-prone daughter a Dramamine before we got going at 5:00 am. I was on it!

Overall, the road trip was fantastic! I heard zero complaints from the backseat. My son said he still likes flying better but didn't get whiny about the trip. It felt miraculous and like a major family accomplishment. While saying yes to the trip may have been spontaneous, everything that came next was an exercise in strategic planning. I made sure I did everything possible to set us up for success.

I had hesitancies and concerns when we said yes to the adventure! I know that some of my friends thought we were taking on too much by taking that 16-hour road trip. All of that is okay! It's totally fine for you to try something new, knowing it may be tough. It's okay to say yes to adventure and then second guess the decision. I hope that you will choose to push your comfort zone every so often! Some of the best made memories are the ones that begin with a brave yes!

Some of the best made memories are the ones that begin with a brave yes!

The memories we built along the coast with my family were incredible! We spent time with family we rarely get to see. My kids rode boats and kayaks, climbed on rocks and visited a lighthouse. We took a day trip to a small island and got to explore and walk on the hull of a shipwreck. The memories we made were beyond precious and are moments I'll cherish forever. I would have been so sad had I sat at home, sticking to the original plan for our summer. I'm thankful for how my faith has changed me over the years, to help me relax a little and let go of the need for tightly knit plans.

Through that experience I learned how important it is to live both strategically and spontaneously. We can be willing to jump on unexpected opportunities while remaining deliberate as to how those opportunities come to fruition. Can you imagine if we went 16 hours without those DVD players or if I forgot to mention watching water intake? Practical solutions and conditions for success still matter—reckless spontaneity is good for no one.

When was the last time you decided to throw caution to the wind and say yes to something that seemed just a little wild? If you can't think of an example perhaps it's time to mentally commit to more spontaneity and unexpected possibilities! If you can bring numerous examples to mind then spend time thinking about all the many ways your spontaneity has enriched and enhanced your life!

A Spontaneous Shake-Up

My colorful career story makes for a great backdrop to detail my "before and after." It isn't only in this context that we need to embrace the contrast of these two competing qualities. A flexible framework is so important as we love our families and those who we hold most dear.

I can call to mind a recent instance in which my ability to be strategic and spontaneous allowed me to come alongside my daughter and help her through a tough day.

She got home from school, and I could tell something was off. She kept telling me school went fine and nothing specific was wrong, but I could see it in her eyes. Something had impacted her mood and emotions—she was down. As the night went on, tears welled up and she expressed feeling sad for an unknown reason. I've been there—I think we all have. All the little things that irritate us and try to pull us down accumulate and we sit heavy, but we also don't fully understand why. Without understanding exactly what is wrong it can feel impossible to make it right.

I hugged her, reassured, tried to help her refocus, but it was all futile. I could tell she was struggling to release it. So, I decided to shake things up for her.

"Get your shoes, we're going out!"

With no heads up or telling her the plan I took her to the Dollar General near our house and we got all sorts of random silly things. The surprise of it all put a smile on her face. As we browsed the aisles, we scooped up an assortment of things we just *had* to have: new fuzzy socks, sour gummy worms, a box of chocolates, and a new set of markers. We giggled as we made our selections of indulgences that we don't normally spontaneously buy. The total cost of the treats was less than $10 and she was visibly lighter as we exited the store. Priceless, right?

The shake-up didn't stop there.

Our next stop was a nearby walking trail. The sun was setting as we began to stroll—but not without first eating a chocolate of our choice. I opted for salted caramel, and she went the strawberry creme route. Sugared up and feeling electrified by our spontaneous outing, she was free.

Whatever had held her down no longer had a hold on her. I watched her skip, laugh, twirl, cartwheel, and slip back into her best self: her joyful, carefree, weightless self. It was beautiful.

With fresh air in our lungs, I watched her hair catch the light from the sunset while she grinned ear to ear. It was everything—*she was everything*. I could tell she felt boundless, and I joined her in that reality. The only words she seemed to have were "I love you mommy." Otherwise, the freedom she felt left her speechless.

I watched her float around that track, lifted by childhood joy. While motherhood often feels so messy and complicated, in that moment it felt sweet and simple. Just me, my girl, and the setting sun.

I don't always get it right as a mom, but that night I did. I reflect on that snapshot moment of our lives and realize it went well because I was strategic and spontaneous at the exact same time. I recognized that my girl was floundering and needed someone to step in and help. I launched a plan to intervene and help her reset. The plan was randomly implemented—a spontaneous outing. Yet, each moment of that outing was intentionally crafted to bring her delight and wash her in feelings of love.

I'm so thankful that although our day was full, I still had space for my girl. We had plans, but she was most important, and I was able to prioritize her.

Keep your eyes open for the chance to be spontaneous and strategic in the way you love others. Don't be such a schedule-stickler that you are unable to grab onto spontaneous opportunities for blessing and vibrancy. If you feel the urge to do something just a little unexpected, go with it! See what kind of memories you can make and bonds you can strengthen as you allow love to guide your decision making. The people we love are so important and the way we show up for them needs to reflect that they are in fact a priority.

Action Item: Within the next week do something silly and spontaneous for the sake of doing something silly and spontaneous. Make it fun and a bit indulgent (which does not have to mean expensive!). Reflect on how it felt and what you gained through the experience.

Living Little by Little

Although I now embrace a lot more spontaneity in my life, I haven't let go of living with intention. I like to be fully aware of each moment, as I take the next right step. The beauty of pairing strategy with a spontaneous way of living is that I can take a determined step forward, maximizing on that moment, without having to worry about where it's ultimately leading me. That's where faith fills in the gap. I'm focused most intently on what God is asking of me today and I'm prayerful about my tomorrows.

Afterall, we are asked to choose our faith daily—not weekly, monthly or yearly.[5] We are also urged to pray for our daily bread, which is asking for all our needs to be met one day at a time.[6] Little by little He leads. Little by little we need to follow. The more we grab onto this truth the less we will fear the future.

One day recently I was struggling to do this. I wasn't following my own advice. I was spiraling into anxiety over a

5. Luke 9:23
6. Matthew 6:11

future situation that was a full year away. I confessed this to my friend and mentor. I shared how I wanted the goal to be met today—not one year from now. As a man of faith, He lovingly pointed me to Exodus 23:29–30 (NIV) to remind me of how God leads. In this account, God promises the wandering Israelites that He will give them their promised land.

> But I will not drive them out in a single year, because the land would become desolate and the wild animals too numerous for you. Little by little I will drive them out before you, until you have increased enough to take possession of the land.

The promised land would be provided in perfect timing in the perfect way. It wasn't just the fact that God was going to do it—He was going to do it in the exact way He knew was best. All the Israelites needed to do was follow God's lead, little by little. They couldn't control or rush the process.

These words were so sweetly convicting in my life. I realized that I was slipping into control-freak tendencies in my fear and anxiety. I realized I needed to trust not only that God would provide but that He would do it in the best way for me and the circumstances. His ways are so much better, higher, and more profound than ours could ever be. Little by little, He leads.

How are you trying to rush the process in your life? How are you being so determined that you are encroaching on God's ability to work wonders on your behalf? Now is a great time for you to resolve to go little-by-little, only taking the next right step until you hear and see additional direction from God.

It can feel scary to let go and release control within our lives. However, when you allow faith to guide you, you can be set free from the need to hold tightly to all the pieces of your life. Trust God with a bold expectation that He will do great things in your life!

Be purpose-driven and open to possibilities in your life. Boldly pursue both strategy and spontaneity.

Brave and Bold Steps Forward

Are you ready to step into what it can mean for your life, if you embrace the reality of being both strategic and spontaneous? I'm confident that you are worth it and wonderful—you've got this!

1. What is an example of a disappointment you've experienced that God was able to redeem?
2. What is an area of your life that you are seeking to control, rather than trusting it in God's hands?
3. What is a practical step you can take to create more space in your days for divine interruptions?
4. Honestly reflect on where you are finding your identity. Is it within your accomplishments and goals or in God?
5. How are you prioritizing people and relationships at work? What about at home?

CHAPTER 4

BROKEN AND WHOLE

I was standing around the office, having a spontaneous stand-up meeting with one of our video producers. It was "back in the day" when I was working for my *alma mater* as an Associate Vice President and spokesperson. Per usual, I was sipping my coffee while we met, and the purpose of that meeting was to identify a student we could feature in an upcoming video segment. We needed someone who is a champion over adversity! The same name came to mind for both of us and I asked, "but do you think she's an over-comer?" The answer I received was simple yet so profound.

"She has too much joy to not have a story."

The fact that my coworker associated joy with struggle stopped me in my tracks. I quickly realized that she was right. Our struggles allow us to develop a redemption story. They give us perspective, depth and dimension. The bad makes us appreciate the good. The darkness provides an opportunity for the light to shine through. Our challenges can be the driving force that instills in us the will to push for joy at all costs. Not happiness—but joy.

Happiness is a temporary state of being. Joy is a steadfast posture of your heart.

Joy does not mean you are ignorant to the difficult things of the world and the struggles faced by many. Rather, despite the hardship, you choose to hope and believe that no amount of turmoil can disrupt God's plans and His sovereignty. Joy is the ultimate act of defiance in a world that is broken by heavy issues and too much sadness.

> Joy is the ultimate act of defiance in a world that is broken by heavy issues and too much sadness.

Do you know what it feels like to be unburdened? You are promised in 2 Corinthians 3:17, "Where the spirit of the Lord is, there is freedom." When you release the things that once held you down you become transformed. You no longer carry guilt, shame, and pain. It doesn't erase that bad things have happened, but it's a glorious reframing of your situation and experiences. One of the most beautiful paradoxes you can embrace is that you can be both broken and whole.

This is your invitation into a place in which the human condition—sickness, sin, abuse, struggle—does not control you but is an integrated part of your story and becomes a reflection of God's power in your life.

Enter into New Hope

There was no better solidifying experience on the value of choosing joy than the first time I traveled to New Hope Girls in the Dominican Republic (DR). New Hope Girls is on a mission to shine light into the darkness within the broken *barrios* (rundown neighborhoods) of the DR.[1] The problems of human trafficking, sexual exploitation and abuse are staggering. However, instead of seeing these problems and feeling hopeless, New Hope sees these problems and chooses to fight back, one girl at a time.

After a girl receives her rescue, New Hope welcomes them into a home in which they receive care for their physical, emotional and faith-based needs. They are loved as daughters and are given nothing but the best—after all, they are daughters of the King.[2] The adult women are provided with dignified employment within the workshop and are paid a living wage to produce high-quality, hand-made fabric purses and bags. Through outreach within the *barrio,* there are efforts to break the systems and traditions that bind so many women and girls within the community. The team is mission-focused and purpose-driven to the core and know the work they are doing is of critical importance.

I met the leader of New Hope, aptly named Joy (and now one of my favorite friends!), while she was visiting our local community in Virginia. After hearing her heart for the ministry and learning details of their work, I knew I wanted to serve and support. The real and raw work at hand beckoned me to join the fight. Even in our first meeting my eyes teared up, my heart swelled with love and longing to engage and join their fight. I found a kindred spirit in Joy and an unshakable sense of connection to New Hope's mission, vision and approach.

---

1. Go learn more at www.NewHopeGirls.com!
2. 1 Peter 2:9

There is no shortage of opportunities to better the world! I hope you will allow yourself to be sensitive to the things that break your heart and hit you in the gut. When you feel the stirring and find yourself beckoned, don't look away! Consider how it could be an invitation to step out to serve, love, and join redemptive work. Be bold in recognizing where you feel led to make an impact in this world.

Impact rarely happens over night! It's in the little-by-little moments when we choose to take the next right step. After more than a year of friendship with Joy, and many "little-by-little" moments, we discussed the possibility of me traveling to the DR to support their marketing efforts and get to know them better. Joy was certain that if I did not travel there, meet the girls, see the *barrio*, interact with her staff, or see the workshop, I would not be able to truly feel the depths of their story.

With my dad by my side, we journeyed to New Hope Girls with the goal of tangibly supporting the work of the organization but without clarity about what that could look like. We flew into Santiago and were met by Joy and her husband Vidal. My past international travel was limited to tourist-areas, so for me, this was an experience like none other. I most certainly stepped outside of my comfort zone.

While in the DR we spent much time in the *barrio* of LaVega. After arriving, it became clear that I could serve them by documenting the voices and stories of the women and children helped by New Hope. We knew that understanding the impact and function of the organization through their eyes was critical for future growth and strategic direction. This work was an incredible honor and it meant that I went physically, emotionally, and spiritually into challenging places.

When I entered the *barrio*, my senses were overwhelmed with the unfamiliar. Music blaring, motorbikes zipping by, people wandering along the sidewalks, and a lingering dust in the air. The smells were foreign and cycled through aromas of food and the odor of decay. Sometimes I would catch a whiff of something burning. Trash was strewn about, and chickens were often wandering up and down alleyways. It was an eyes-wide-open and immersive experience.

I've never used my skills and talents in such an emotionally intense way! I quickly became comfortable working with a continuous stream of tears running down my face. As I interviewed the caregivers of the girls, I finally stopped to let them know that even though I couldn't stop crying, I *really* was okay. I shared that my tears helped me feel and there was no reason to censor their stories on my behalf. So, they spoke, Joy translated, and my tears fell.

It was painful to hear what the women and girls have endured. They are God's beautiful creation but have been treated like an object to be used and abused. They have been hurt and broken in nearly every sense of the word. And yet, between the flow of tears there was laughter. We cackled as the women lovingly teased each other and recalled funny stories that juxtaposed the pain. It was in those sweet and simple moments that I witnessed how we can exist fully in the tension between all that is broken and whole.

During my time in the DR, I heard stories riddled with suffering, starvation, sexual abuse and abandonment. Girls as young as four needed rescuing. Children who will forever bear physical scars from what they have endured—and the emotional scars invisible to the eye.

These personal narratives were set in the most painful places. However, I also heard stories that were filled with hope and light. These girls and women realize that the brokenness they have experienced does not define them. They have untouchable worth! The redemption story they personify, rooted in unwavering faith in God, sets them free from the darkness that once tried to own them. They laugh, smile and celebrate. Together, they walk through the shadows and step into the light.

One day in particular was the embodiment of broken and whole—sorrow and joy. I spent most of the day deep in the *barrio* interviewing women who have been impacted by hardship and pain but have overcome it—and continue to fight to overcome it. I was honored to be able to enter their homes, meet their babies and hear their personal journeys. They had so little, but everywhere I went they generously offered their stories to me.

After a long day in the *barrio* my dad and I returned to the home we were staying in—complete with iron bars on all the windows. We did our best to clean up, put on the one "fancy" outfit we brought and join the girls in the safe home for a celebration. It was Maria's[3] *quinceañera*.

A *quinceañera* is a critical milestone within Dominican culture and is a rite of passage as one goes from being a girl to a woman. Wow, Maria was radiant that night! She entered the party in a beautiful gown, wearing high heels for the first time and adorned in makeup with a fancy hair style. Truly the most beautiful part was the smile stretched across her face. She was radiant! She received a gift of a Bible, and everyone spoke blessings over her life.

---

3. Note: Name changed to respect her identity and story.

Hearing all the voices, from the youngest to the oldest, speak over Maria was everything to me. It was surreal. These girls have every earthly reason in the world to choose misery, shame, and resentment for the things that have been done to them. Instead, they have chosen God's truth about who they are!

As the night evolved, we enjoyed a meal, cake, dancing, and music. The girls had several choreographed songs they tried to teach me, and we spent time looking up at the *estrellas* together. It was an out-of-body and magical moment that is forever etched in my heart.

Within one day, I had heard stories of the ultimate lows within our broken world and then contrasted it by experiencing jubilation and celebration. I encountered an immersive reality of being broken and beautifully whole.

The girls and women of New Hope affix their identity to Jesus. They know that He transforms them and redeems them.

Certainly, one could look at their lives and feel bad for them because of all that they have experienced. However, I look at their lives and feel overwhelmed by the power of their redemption story. Their rescue is not just a physical rescue but is a soul-level rescue that invites them to rest assured in their true identity.

I'm reminded that even within the most lost, destitute, and dark place there is still hope that we can step back into a place illuminated and bright. There is no place too far gone—this true for our girls in the Dominican Republic and this is true for you.

The wholeness and wholeheartedness that the girls and women of New Hope embrace is not without significant work. It also comes with setbacks at times. The New Hope team of caregivers and therapists use trauma-informed therapy to help girls overcome—and continue to overcome—the violence, abuse and trauma of the past. It's a process wrapped in faith, and the finish line is ever changing. It takes long-term dedication and a commitment to seeking wholeness regardless of how fragmented the pieces may feel and how many setbacks may be experienced. It also takes a community committed to joining each other in the fight—every single day.

Do you know what it feels like to experience a setback in your own journey? It could be that you felt like you had made major strides toward feeling whole and then out of nowhere, you are triggered and feel like so much precious progress has been lost. Don't dismay and please extend yourself grace. Healing and pursuing wholeness are anything but straightforward. Persevere through those moments that feel so disheartening and trust that your trajectory is pushing you forward. Please stay the course.

My first trip to visit New Hope has left such a lasting impact on me. I cherish the notes and transcripts of the interviews from my first trip to the DR. One caregiver spoke such beautiful words that I realized are for all of us:

I have hope in the girls. I can see the potential. I just know that God has huge and marvelous plans. God loves them. God takes care of them. God sees them as a precious jewel. My hope is that they learn to see themselves like that and that they can receive that kind of love. That's our work.

I will take her words and say this to you: My hope is that you learn to see yourself as a precious jewel. That you see your potential and know that God has huge and marvelous plans for your life. My heart's desire for you is that you will not define yourself by the broken pieces but will allow God to enter in and make you whole.

Brokenness can come as the result of trauma or abuse. As a police officer, I saw far too much of this. I saw how without intervention and resources, the wrongs of the past can

> My hope is that you learn to see yourself as a precious jewel. That you see your potential and know that God has huge and marvelous plans for your life.

become more complex and challenging, stealing joy and purpose in its wake. We all have aspects of our past, or perhaps current realities, that are laced with painful emotions. But we can all choose to own our story moving forward.

Some journeys appear more painful and challenging than others, but everyone has heavy moments they still wrestle with carrying. You cannot insulate yourself from the bad, but you can choose to see the good. Heartache, death, divorce, lost jobs, changing friendships, health problems—these are not things anyone can fully control and yet they are things so many people face. They are also things that can make you feel broken. Deep moments of pain can make you feel like your foundation is starting to crumble.

Feeling broken is not always a chronic condition or associated with a major trauma or one specific incident. Day to day living can be exhausting, overwhelming and damaging. There are days that I head home and the weight of responsibility, expectations and needs feel like more than I can handle. Do you know that feeling? If someone asked you, "What's wrong?" you may not have a good answer because it's the culmination of all the little things.

I know that sometimes I push myself so hard that I accumulate more emotional stress than I can handle and have a temporary "meltdown" (as we lovingly call them in our home). I can think of more than one example where I got home from work just to walk upstairs, put on my sweats and sit on the floor of our closet for an ugly cry. While not a pretty experience, it becomes necessary from time to time.

This kind of little-by-little brokenness reminds me of a stress fracture. It's not caused by a major catastrophic incident but the small and sneaky moments where life is just too much. Over time, your soul becomes weary as you shoulder the daily burdens and demands. The pressure to succeed at work, look perfect, raise great kids, have a fantastic marriage, keep a clean house, and make time for fun can really add up. The volume of expectations, self-imposed or otherwise, can be way too much.

You were not designed to bear the burdens the world hefts upon us without any kind of release or soul refresh. Please hear me loud and hear me clear: you are not defined by your brokenness, nor should you be consumed by it. You can be unburdened. There is a path forward and your brokenness is not the full story.

> There is a path forward and your brokenness is not the full story.

We're All Messy

Do you feel messy? I know that I have so many moments and days where I'm very aware of all the shortcomings, hang ups, mistakes, and rough edges in my life.

I bet you have those moments too.

We all seem to have mastered the skill of making things look good on social media. However, I know that in between my highlights there are times I feel like I'm flirting with emotional disaster with each tentative step I take.

I wonder if you also have moments in which you teeter on the line of overwhelm, "too much" and burn out? I know that it helps me tremendously to have friends I can process with when I'm feeling extra messy! Hearing someone affirm that they know the feeling or have been there too is such a source of comfort when I feel like I must be the only one in shambles.

When you can identify safe places for sharing, confessing and affirming truth you will be better for it. The ruse that you have it all together is one of the most deceptive and alienating lies you can tell yourself or others. None of us, in this broken world, can escape the bumps, bruises and deep cuts of humanity. But you can honestly share and allow others to come alongside you in truth, encouragement and love.[4]

When God describes the people of His church, He uses the analogy of the body.[5] Each part having a function and role, with Jesus as the head. You have a role to play and ways you can mutually pursue strength and unity—even in your struggles. As 1 Corinthians 12:26 shares, "If one member suffers, all suffer together; if one member is honored, all rejoice together." Let's cry together, laugh together, and join together!

Let's commit to sharing in the joys and struggles— our brokenness and our wholeness—together.

> Let's commit to sharing in the joys and struggles—our brokenness and our wholeness—together.

---

4. Hebrews 3:13
5. 1 Corinthians 12:12–27

I have found that both my struggle with infertility and my battle with melanoma have provided countless opportunities to connect with others in deep and encouraging ways. I feel gratitude for the journey and my opportunity to overcome challenges along the way. I want to own the tough aspects and use them to uplift others in similarly challenging times. I value offering both practical advice and general feedback about how others may also approach their challenges.

Consider if you have endured hardships and struggles that will give you the unique opportunity to love others well. There is something impactful about connecting with a person who can honestly say, "I've been there too." Think about if you are living openly with your hardships, allowing them to be a blessing to others. The beauty of that open handed living is that your hardship will start to be reframed in the wake of the purpose it now has.

I remember the day my dear friend and mentor left me a voicemail sharing that she had just received a cancer diagnosis. Wow. That news hit hard. It was on the front end of

> Your hardship will start to be reframed in the wake of the purpose it now has.

the Covid-19 pandemic and so much felt out of control. I was able to encourage my friend that it's normal to cycle through a myriad of emotions, often all within five minutes. I explained how processing a major medical diagnosis is like doing mental gymnastics. She knew that I had battled melanoma and have been very open about that health struggle. In her phone call she expressed hope that I'd be able to listen, offer advice, and approach the conversation with informed perspective.

It was a blessing that the pain and fear I once experienced were transformed into an opportunity to come alongside someone I love and support her through her dark time. God is so good like that. He allows our struggle to be used to love others and to show the impact our faith has on our lives.

You serve no one well by holding tight to your challenges. Your willingness to own what is or was once broken gives others permission to do the same. You set a new norm within your circles that sharing the tough stuff is safe and even welcome. Your authenticity gives others freedom to share their own struggles. As Henry David Thoreau poetically noted, "We all live quiet lives of desperation" and are eager to be seen, heard, affirmed and supported. Show others that you are there for them as a present and a willing thinking-partner. Live in a way that demonstrates you are eager to support and listen. Be ready to walk through the tough stuff and stubbornly claim joy.

> As Henry David Thoreau poetically noted, "We all live quiet lives of desperation" and are eager to be seen, heard, affirmed and supported. Show others that you are there for them as a present and a willing thinking partner.

Remember how I worry about you? Please know that if you are wrestling with pain, I want you to get help. I get deeply concerned for friends who are unable to acknowledge the challenges they are experiencing and who don't seek support.

A powerful step toward choosing resiliency is asking for help, even professional help, when needed. Proverbs tells us that it's wise to seek counsel, in a number of different places.[6] As you seek counsel and support, it's important to remember that ultimately your aims should be to allow God to guide your every step and for Him to renew your spirit. Counselors can be one tool or method by which He does exactly that!

> You have an untouchable worth and value that no amount of brokenness can impact.

It's a courageous choice and a wonderful option to bring formal support systems into your life to weather the toughest seasons and most painful elements of your past and present. Many churches have counselors or formal programs to help provide that support. There are also trained mental health professionals who love the Lord and can offer practical and faith-informed wisdom for how you can fight the challenges and pain in your life.

Your mental, physical and spiritual well-being are all intricately connected. Prayerfully take the steps needed to ensure you are well supported and can shine whole. Remember that God is the one who controls your story. You have an untouchable worth and value that no amount of brokenness can impact.

> Action Item: Think of a hard situation or experience you have overcome. How can you use your testimony to encourage others and lift them up within their own struggles? Spend time thinking about how your broken pieces can be used to love and serve others.

6. Proverbs 13:10 & Proverbs 24:6

Self-Care and Soul-Care

Using constructive means to cope is the goal for long-term wellness and the perfect pairing of broken and whole. This creates a strong foundation so if things go sideways you are facing adversity from a place of strength. You create conditions to succeed in the long-term by putting in the wellness work each day.

Our culture is saturated with talk of self-care. It's common knowledge that the *struggle is real*—and shared. There is no shortage of books, podcasts, blogs, Instagram posts and websites dedicated to coaching you into your most optimized life that is laced in self-care. God did indeed create physical bodies that require care, like exercise and plenty of rest. There are undoubtedly very tangible ways you can take care of yourself and help yourself feel a greater sense of calm and wellness.

When my kids were really little, I used to love taking a half-day off from work to escape to an afternoon movie. Being alone, in the dark, with a cherry slushy and a big container of extra buttery popcorn took indulgence to a whole new level. My mind would disappear into the plot of the movie, and I would emerge feeling renewed by the experience. It was just what I needed to feel recharged and ready to embrace the realities of motherhood again. Sometimes buttery popcorn is the healthiest thing we can do for ourselves! If you are a nutritionist reading this just know that I'm kidding (well, only kind of kidding).

For each of us, *the thing* that does the trick is going to vary but we need to each be astutely aware of what it takes to rejuvenate our minds and bodies. We need to proactively pursue mental wellness and be uncompromising in our commitment

> Being proactive in both your physical and mental self-care honors the mind and body given to you by God.

to it. Being proactive in both your physical and mental self-care honors the mind and body given to you by God.

While those practical and physical methods are important and should be tended to, you cannot overlook the need for proactive soul-care. This is the faith-oriented component of self-care that goes so much deeper than your workout schedule, nutritional plan, or commitment to a relaxing bath at the end of the day.

God graciously provided you with a model for what soul-care looks like. You can see Jesus live out soul-care throughout the accounts of His life, within scripture.

"And rising very early in the morning, while it was still dark, He departed and went out to a desolate place, and there He prayed."[7]

Jesus had so much important work before Him—His ministry and the cross—and yet Jesus never neglected to be in intimate conversation with God. He gave you a clear example of what it looks like to put in the daily work of seeking quiet time and His priorities were made known

> Jesus had so much important work before Him—His ministry and the cross—and yet Jesus never neglected to be in intimate conversation with God.

based on how He began each day. Close your eyes and imagine Jesus quietly slipping away to claim His moment with the Lord. Don't forget to claim your moment, too!

7. Mark 1:35

I'm a morning person and also love to rise early, often while it's still dark. With bleary eyes and the promise of a new day I make my way to my favorite spot on the couch. As my mind unlocks and becomes clear, I connect deeply with God. In the quiet, I'm able to hear Him. I allow this time to frame out how the rest of the day will go. It's foundational as a first-things-first approach. My brain grabs onto truth without distraction and interruption. That kind of soul-care is so critical for me as a woman of faith. It's how I ensure I'm battle-ready for the day.

What about you? What time and space are you holding for the most important work—the soul work? How are you taking steps to strengthen your spirit, so that when the brokenness strikes you will be strong and battle ready? Not only is this a way to refresh when the demands and darkness are too much. Entering into your day like this is a proactive approach to fighting despair, hopelessness and burnout.

Beyond the first part of my day, I find that I regularly need to recalibrate as my days evolve. I half-jokingly describe this as my quest to "get right with the Lord" as the hustle and bustle grabs ahold of me.

Picture this—I'm sitting at my desk, focused on a task. Then my email alerts and I read an incredibly disappointing message. Something I had hoped for has fallen through. I immediately feel myself going to a place of anger and discouragement. The bubbling up of anger is my cue that it's time to fight back. I rise from my desk, go outside into the fresh air, and pray about all the yucky feelings I have inside. I instantly start to recalibrate to grab onto a faith perspective.

In that small break, I'm actively applying the scripture that instructs us to take every thought captive.[8]

Can you think of a recent example where your day was going swimmingly wonderful—until it wasn't? You were sweetly sailing along and then all of a sudden started sinking? How did you react and respond to the frustrating or infuriating circumstances? Do you feel like you were able to take every thought captive, or did you find yourself indulging the anger?

> **Action Item:** Identify a situation where you let your emotions take control of you and frame the situation. What were the outcomes? Now, take a moment to consider how the story could have evolved differently if you had submitted your feelings to the Lord.

I can think of numerous situations where I failed to trust my emotions and circumstances to God. I can't think of a single time that it served me well to go that route. Conversely, I can also think of situations where I submitted the entirety of my mess to Him with confidence He will take care of it. When I go that route, He never lets me down.

That is a lesson I continue to learn as a deep-feeling, highly emotional person. Are you a deep feeler too? Sometimes I think being like this gets viewed as a weakness. I actually love being this way! However, without care and awareness, it can go places it shouldn't. I can be tempted to indulge my emotions and let them set the tone for my days, rather than the one who is the Maker of my days.

A recent hardship within my family really forced me to confront this head on. I was wrestling, lamenting and fighting

---

8. 2 Corinthians 10:5

with so many negative feelings. Sadness, fear, insecurity and even feeling rejected.

Instead of letting it go, I laid with it. You know what I mean? I laid my head on the pillow and my mind raced round and round on all the "what ifs" and "maybes" and started to have hypothetical conversations with everyone involved in the situation. I allowed the possibilities to play out in my mind, keeping me from sleep and robbing me of peace. I was consumed and unsure of how to let it go.

There may be something you can call to mind that you have laid with recently, an issue that you couldn't stop considering from every possible angle and that kept your mind racing when it should be resting. Recognize right now that it's time to take those thoughts captive!

In my situation, I became painfully aware of how tightly I was clinging to the broken. I realized I was wrapping my arms around my pain and refusing to let God come in and transform it. In a weird way I wanted to sit with the pain and had become way too friendly with it. I was able to recognize it was unhealthy and that I had to figure out a way to release it.

I went on a run and wrestled with God. Tears streaming down my face, I ran with all my might. I knew that the run wasn't just about moving my body, it was about taking my emotions captive and finally releasing the heartache. As I ran, I began saying out loud, "Take it God. Take it. I can't carry it anymore."

I'm sure to a passerby I looked insane. But to God, I know I looked beautiful. I was finally surrendering

I'm sure to a passerby I looked insane. But to God, I know I looked beautiful.

all of the pain and hurt I was carrying. At last, I was trusting God to actually be God in this area of my life. I quit trying to be my own self-controlling god and stopped believing I could fix this on my own. I released it. I let it go. And in that moment, I was free.

In the coming days I felt lighter. When my head hit the pillow, I didn't have a broken record of worry and despair. I left it at the track that day. Though there were moments where the pain would begin to stir again, I would remind myself, "you left that at the track." It served as a physical place where I could visualize leaving the pain. I also shared this experience with my husband and some of my closest friends. I asked them to hold me accountable in the future with the simple question, "I thought you left that at the track?" It was my cue to remember how I decided on that day to give God the control that is rightfully His.

What do you need to leave at the track? Are you overdue for a wrestling match with the Lord, one in which you pour out your pain? Take brave steps forward in trusting God to handle your emotions. He is big enough; He can take it. Your honest tears and heartfelt cries are beautiful to Him. I urge you to stop trying to be the god of your emotions and pain. It's time to release because you were never meant to carry it in the first place.

> Take brave steps forward in trusting God to handle your emotions. He is big enough; He can take it.

It could be that you also need to find a place of solitude where you can go wrestle with the pain and then commit to leaving it there. For me, it was a track. For you, it could be a walking path, a coffee shop, alongside a stream, or in your own backyard. I love how having a physical place associated with the release is a forever reminder. A landmark of healing and also accountability.

A physical place can represent an accountability landmark, but don't neglect the accountability of sharing with others. Consider how those closest to you can hold you accountable to replacing your unhealthy inner dialogue with truth and goodness. I want so badly for you to feel the loving support of friends and family. In my perfect world the words you would hear them speak over you are this: "You are worth it, you are wonderful, and this was never yours to carry—so let it go."

Love Anyway

Being hurt and feeling broken can cause you to hold back and live in a constant state of defense. Instead of flinging your arms wide open and greeting a new day you may turn inward, hugging yourself, protecting your heart. Please don't live that way.

Constantly attempting to protect yourself from hurt and pain will not change circumstances. It will however change you and your ability to live a vibrant life. There's no judgment if this is where you find yourself right now, or if you know you've lived like this in the past. It seems to be one expression of a fight or flight response, emotional barricades. Instead of being willing to fight the darkness we retreat deep inside ourselves.

My work with New Hope Girls has really challenged me to consider if I'm living in an openhearted way, despite the heartbreak. What began as a one-time trip to New Hope Girls, has evolved into something so much more immersive and beautiful! Four years after that initial trip, I left my role as an Associate Vice President at a mid-sized university and RSVPed to God's invitation for more.

I now work stateside with specific responsibilities for growing the workshop component of our organization. The workshop is where our adult women make gorgeous bags that not only help them provide for their families but also help fund the rescue and refuge of our girls. This is a social entrepreneurship role that pulls from all the different career stops along the way.

Most days, my work is marked by hope, healing and an abundance of joy! We get to celebrate job creation, lives restored, and dreams achieved. I get a front row seat to watch little girls who were once enveloped in darkness, walk tall. Women and girls alike are piercing the darkness with their light each and every day. Yes, yes and YES.

In contrast, working for New Hope Girls and being all-in means sometimes I have days that come with emotional gut punches. Some aren't just a gut punch but are a sucker punch. I felt it when I heard the words, "She's going home."

Out of nowhere, my sweet little *amiguita* from New Hope Girls was being removed from our home to live with a family member. This is not the norm, and it was nothing we saw coming. However, the legal system fully cleared it, and an order was in hand. We were shocked and sent reeling. There was nothing we could do. Her family was on their way to get her and take her home. Far away from her home with us was a home with them.

If you knew her story and where she'd come from, you wouldn't want her to go back either. You wouldn't fully trust that this really was in her best interest. And yet, the system had decided.

So, there I sat. Three plane rides and an ocean between us, no way to get there and hug her goodbye. No opportunity to look her in her eyes, and in my broken Spanish affirm the depths of my love for her. I knew I was going to have to trust in a greater plan than either of us could control.

Just like that, my sweet little friend, and a person I had come to know, love, and care for, was no longer part of my life. Because of infrastructure, systems, and "the way things are," it wasn't like she was just moving down the street and we could become pen pals. Although I know our team will do their best to keep tabs on her and find ways to check in, she is in essence totally gone from my world. She is in the wind.

The loss came without the luxury of a real goodbye. The lingering reminders of her will be the letters she wrote, the pictures we took together, and the memory of her sweet smile etched into my mind's eye. I can still hear her voice and will never forget the time she shared her testimony of transformation—of the terrible places God had delivered her from.

When I processed the pain of losing my sweet friend and all the heartache that came with it, my initial thought was to be more careful next time. In the unexpected and jarring pain, I found myself strategizing on how I could protect myself from future pain by loving a little less immersively next time.

Have you found yourself so hurt that you immediately began making promises about how you'd toughen up, harden your heart, and proactively put defense systems up? I wonder if your reaction to pain is withdrawing with a vow that you'll never allow it to hurt like that again. Initially, that's what I wanted to do.

I considered running from my sadness and thought about holding back just a little more next time. Maybe if I loved less, it would hurt less? But that is a foolish approach and desolate way of living. Love is not meant to be approached with a scarcity mindset, as if at any moment it will all disappear and there will no longer be enough.

Love is meant to be a cannonball in the pool on a hot summer day, all in and enveloped. I want to love in *that* way. I also want the same for you. I want you to delight in the joy of vibrant love that can celebrate every moment, without living with the fear of what could go wrong. Let the love you feel for others move you and don't let the hurts of the past rob you of future joy. Afterall, I can love this way and you can love this way because God first loved us in this immersive, "all the way in" kind of way.[9]

> God first loved us in this immersive, "all the way in" kind of way.

Please don't put up a fortress around your heart because of past pain. This world will be ugly and may break your heart—love anyway. God *commanded* us to love Him and love others. You heard right. It wasn't a polite suggestion; it was a command to love.[10]

In your ability to love deeply, your heart will be transformed. You will grow through the pain and experience love with more brilliance than you could have, had you stayed insulated within yourself. If things were broken, you will find healing. If you felt lonely in your pain, you will find community. If you felt lost, love will help guide you back.

Remember, love is the greatest of all.

When you feel the temptation to run from relationships and protect yourself from pain, I urge you not to. Love anyway. Embrace people and celebrate their impact in your life. Don't

---

9. John 3:16
10. Matthew 22:36–40

try to shield yourself or live small—throw your arms wide open with big, big love. Choose relational bravery in the face of brokenness and a bold spirit of love.

> Remember, love is the greatest of all.

As I sit here, thinking about my sweet friend from New Hope Girls, and the sudden goodbye, I realize that knowing her has brought such depth and beauty to my life. The tears still fall when I think of her, but I trust her into God's hands and know that, as much as I love her, He loves her infinitely more than me.

Beauty in the Ashes

God has the most wonderful way of turning our ashes into beauty.[11] He takes all of our broken pieces and turns them into a masterpiece, in only a way that our He can do. In Romans 8:28 we are promised "... that for those who love God all things work together for good, for those who are called according to his purpose."

Feeling whole in the face of heartache requires a brave and bold faith. It requires the courage to ask for help, belief that you are worth fighting for and intentional steps toward healing and wholeness. Above all, it requires leaning into your faith and releasing the pain you are clutching. Unburden yourself in the Father. He promises to help you carry all that hurts.[12]

> Unburden yourself in the Father. He promises to help you carry all that hurts.

---

11. Isaiah 61:3
12. Matthew 11:28–30

Fall in love with the idea of seeing your life as a beautiful mosaic, lovingly and intentionally crafted. It honors the masterpiece that you are. A masterpiece composed of disparate pieces, experiences, challenges, pain, tears, laughter, joy, and victory all brought together to make something meaningful. While there are clear lines of fracture, some rough edges, color and vibrancy, order and disorder, the big picture is beautiful and complete. It's broken and whole.

There is a bittersweetness to life that you must own and acknowledge. That bittersweetness is your yearning for a perfect world that you simply can't experience this side of heaven. The world is broken, but it can still be beautiful. Life is not all good, nor all bad. There are blessings within even the most arduous aspects of our journey. It does not have to be perfect to be wonderful.

We are all bruised. We have all had our messes, mistakes, losses and challenges. But through the bruises and hard times we can rise whole. This is possible because of how Jesus rose whole, defeating death, darkness and sadness once and for all.

Much of life is out of your control, but there is tremendous beauty in your ability to rise from the ashes and shine bright, lavished in God's abundant grace upon grace.

> There is tremendous beauty in your ability to rise from the ashes and shine bright, lavished in God's abundant grace upon grace.

There are far too many things you cannot change, but you can make a choice about how you will frame life's circumstances both now and in the future. Rather than trying to cover up our bruises, choose to invite God into the parts that hurt as you move forward in strength and beauty. Choose to be broken and whole.

Brave and Bold Steps Forward

Are you ready to step into what it means to intentionally embrace being broken and whole? I know you are brave enough to do this.

1. As you reflect on the paradox of being broken and whole, which word do you feel most describes you in this current season?
2. What practical steps do you need to take to practice better self-care (physical, tangible things)? What about steps toward better soul-care?
3. What hard parts of your life can you use to bless others? How can you allow God to redeem them for His glory?
4. What is a hurt or heartache that you need to actively release to God? How can you "leave it at the track?"
5. How have you witnessed God make beauty for ashes—in your life or in the life of someone close to you?

CHAPTER 5

CAREER FOCUSED AND FAMILY FOCUSED

My career journey has been a joyful (and wild!) journey full of plot twists, pivots, opportunities and hard work. I won't speak in hyperbole and say I have loved *every* minute of it, but I have loved *nearly every* minute of it. More than that, I can confidently say I have loved the overall trajectory and am able to reflect on all my experiences with gratitude.

God makes me giggle when I think of the creative ways He has made sense of such varied experiences. He truly has made my paths straight,[1] even though to some it appears my career trajectory has ping ponged around. Who knew a former cop could take a dramatic pivot and find a meaningful career in marketing and entrepreneurship?

While blessing me with a fun and exciting career adventure, God has simultaneously poured out blessings in the area

---

1. Proverbs 3:5-6

of family. The reality is that my career journey cannot be parsed out from my family journey. They are tightly interwoven, one contributing to or shaping the other at each and every step. There has been both a tension-filled and symbiotic relationship between my work outside the home and my work within our home. I wonder if the same has been true for you.

When it comes to the competing priorities of family and career there is perhaps no more polarizing personal issue for women. It can get downright icky at times.

Women who feel called to stay home and work solely within their homes may wrestle with guilt over not directly contributing to the family income or not doing "more" with their lives. Women who feel called to work outside the home may feel guilt over not being present all the time or seemingly prioritizing income over their kids. I sincerely wish we could all join together—regardless of our career and family choices—and make a universal pinky promise to let all that guilt go.

> I sincerely wish we could all join together—regardless of our career and family choices—and make a universal pinky promise to let all that guilt go.

The struggle can look different for each woman. For more seasoned and mature women it might mean balancing a vibrant career and caring for an aging parent. Other times, it's balancing work with the needs of a sibling or loved one who is going through an immense struggle.

No matter your family dynamic, I feel certain that you have experienced tension between your career and family. I'm here to tell you, and affirm, you can be an amazing career woman and an amazing family woman. You don't have to be one or the other, you don't have to choose between the two. You have the ability to be family focused and career focused.

As I reflect on the plot twists of my life, I realize that across all seasons and job changes I have fought extremely hard to be both family focused and career focused. The fight has not been an easy one, but I firmly believe God has not called me to cut corners in either sphere of my life.

The ability to have a thriving career alongside a marriage and motherhood experience that are equally rich and meaningful comes with challenges. To be blunt, some days it seems impossible and unfair. Choosing to be great in both areas requires a tremendous amount of will, want, intention—and prayer. It requires intentionality and effort. However, the investment you make when you push through the challenges comes with the most beautiful return.

I've loved realizing that my primary ministry is found within the four walls of our home, as I nurture and guide our children alongside my wonderful husband. It's our priority to help our children walk in truth.[2] I know that leading and loving our children is one of the most beautiful ways we can impact this world for good. We are aiming to raise our kids in scripture-informed ways that provide a lifelong faith foundation.

While I'm certain of my calling within the walls of my home, I'm also certain that God is also inviting me to be a blessing within the workplace. I have loved seeing how He creatively uses my passions, gifts, skills, and experiences to bring glory to Him. This has happened within every single

---

2. 3 John 1:4

career context, even the ones that would not appear to be "ministry" in nature.

You are called to be a light everywhere you go, even in your workplace. Afterall, the ministry of Jesus was about entering into everyday experiences, loving deeply, sharing truth, and pointing to the Father every chance He could get. He even encountered people in their places of work, from fishermen to tax collectors.

> You are called to be a light everywhere you go, even in your workplace.

In whatever role you may currently occupy you have the opportunity to shine bright. You can conduct yourself in a way that makes people curious about why you are so thoughtful, considerate, and marked by integrity. That light they are sensing is your faith-shaped way of living. You can pray over coworkers (with them or for them) and you can lift them up before the Lord. You can also embody a work ethic that reflects a belief that it is God Himself you are working for.[3]

One of the biggest career and family struggles I fight is related to my ability to be present. It's often not my physical presence that I struggle with but it's being mentally all-in. Often, I find that my mind likes to continue the workday, long after the clock hits 5:00. No doubt, this makes me a strong employee and committed team member. However, it is important that my family not get my second best or diluted attention. When it's their time, I want to be present for them!

---

3. Colossians 3:23-34

Even though that is my intent, I find my hands magnetically drawn to my cell phone and all the fantastic apps that let me check in to work. Did New Hope Girls get another big order? Have I gotten an email from my amazing publisher? Did my boss reach out with a question? I really struggle to shut my mind down and walk away.

But it matters.

It matters that you and I draw boundaries around our time and hold space for our families. Similarly, it matters that while we are at work, we are also able to draw boundaries around our time and acknowledge that the space is held for work related tasks. Trying to live with one foot in both places at the same time is not healthy or helpful. This is a situation in which you started to get pulled into a split.

To combat this, put accountability measures in place to make sure you are giving yourself conditions to succeed. Leave your phone in your purse and set email notifications to silent. That way the magnetic pull of your email will not draw you in. Communicate with your family about which workplace interruptions make sense and which ones should wait until the workday is over. They should help support your efforts to be both excellent as a family-focused woman and as a career-focused woman.

You've got this, I know you do! I know that you can fight for a career that is life-giving and a family that brings you joy. Your career is a blessing and so is your family. Make sure you handle them with care that reflects your awareness of the blessings.

My Journey to Motherhood

When I met my husband, and could tell he was *the one*, we talked early on about a desire to have a family. We even agreed that we wanted to start a family soon after marriage and that two kids was going to be the perfect number to complete our family. We both agreed that being active parents, who were hands on with our family, was important to us both. I loved dreaming alongside him, imagining him tossing a football with our kids or helping them with homework. I knew he was going to be a fantastic father, and I was right!

I'll never forget the day I found out we were pregnant. I was visiting a new doctor after another (allegedly) failed round of fertility treatments. Our doctor at the time told us ovulation did not happen, and for another month pregnancy was not possible. The bottom line was that the medication would need to be increased. Another cycle of disappointment had washed over us. My anxieties were enhanced as I began wondering "if" we'd be able to get pregnant instead of "when" we'd be able to get pregnant.

I was really struggling emotionally on the current dosage of medication so the reality of increasing it felt impossible. I truly didn't know how I could handle what the journey was asking of me. I had already filled the prescription for my next round of medications and was anticipating the next pill with overwhelming dread. My sister Rose, who was in medical school at the time, strongly encouraged me to get a second opinion before beginning the next round of medicine. She accompanied me to the appointment because I needed some sister-support as the emotional weight of struggling to conceive was becoming too heavy to carry *alone*.

When I arrived at the office, I felt gut-punched when they asked me to provide a urine sample for a pregnancy test. After all, I was there because we weren't able to get pregnant and I had been explicitly told that pregnancy was not possible that month. I remember feeling a sense of sadness with a hint of anger as I complied.

As I sat in my scratchy paper gown in the exam room, I was hopeful that this new physician may have a fresh approach to try. My stomach was in knots because I was eager for a possible path forward. After a quick knock the door opened. The doctor walked in, extended her hand, and said, "Congratulations, you are pregnant."

The jubilation that washed over my soul was beautifully overwhelming. Intense tears of gratitude sprang from my eyes and didn't stop for the entire appointment. Not exaggerating, I walked out the front doors *still* crying tears of joy. The blessing we had hoped and prayed for had happened.

What one doctor had told me was impossible God proved was possible. That is who He is and that is what He does.

> What one doctor had told me was impossible God proved was possible. That is who He is and that is what He does.

That miracle pregnancy resulted in our first born, a precious girl who is brilliant and beautiful, inside and out. We were so fortunate that after having our daughter we were blessed with a son 22 months later. He's the sweetest, most cuddly and imaginative little guy. He completed our family and doubled my capacity to love.

I celebrate the privilege of motherhood and the gift of getting to get to know these two distinct and uniquely different people in such an up-close way. I love that I have a front row seat to their growth, development and adventures. I love being a mom.

When I dreamed about holding our children in my arms, and while we struggled to make that a reality, I didn't let go of my dreams of a vibrant and meaningful career. I wanted both.

The Merits of Career Motherhood

Motherhood is beautiful, fulfilling, and a blessed responsibility. It's also not the only way to be defined as a woman. It can be a beautiful facet to who you are as a person. It's an awe-inspiring and a humbling role that undoubtedly comes with challenges and growth. However, if you allow yourself to be exclusively defined by this special responsibility and role, you are rooting your identity in the wrong thing. Your worth is not rooted in any other person on this planet, to include your children.

> Motherhood is beautiful, fulfilling, and a blessed responsibility. It's also not the only way to be defined as a woman.

Children will misbehave. They will be the reason for gray hair. They will grow in increasing independence as life unfolds. There are times they will break your heart and they will keep you up at night, for one reason or another. All of this is normal and real. With all of this in mind, if you tether your sense of self to your role as a mother you run the risk of feeling like a failure or lost.

If your identity is rooted in your children, it means that you are allowing their choices—good and bad—to dictate your sense of self. That's not how you are asked to define who you are as a woman of faith. You answer to Jesus first, and can find your true identity in Him. After that, you can prioritize the ministry and blessed work of nurturing your family.

Your career is not an exclusive way to determine your identity, either. It can be so exciting to see how work-related tasks and projects can set you on fire. It's fun to see how your God-give talents and passions can be applied to your career. There is something satisfying about others seeing you accomplish great things and shine. However, positions change. Sometimes companies are restructured. New leaders are hired who change the dynamics within a workplace. Even the most stable career or job can be met with unexpected change.

If you root your identity in your career you are anchoring yourself to something that is very temporary. It may be incredibly beautiful and important work! I know there are jobs like that out there because I presently have one like that with New Hope Girls. However, you have to balance your dedication and commitment with the awareness that if you resigned from your job today, they would be able to find a replacement. If you are a small business owner and you shut your doors today, people would find someone else to provide the product or service you provide. Even the most important job is still work—your worth and value transcends your title and position.

> If you root your identity in your career you are anchoring yourself to something that is very temporary.

Your career and your role with your family can come together in a symbiotic way that mutually blesses.

I see my career as a way to inspire my children toward greatness. I'm currently a monthly guest on a regional news show and my kids love watching my segments back, helping me pick outfits for the next segment, or giving input on topics. They are in it with me! Which I'm thankful for. I want them to watch my career unfold and consider opportunities for their own lives. It also matters to me that they see the way my work challenges me and simultaneously allows me to bless others. My career is an ever-evolving adventure and I want them along for the ride!

The first time my family joined me for an adventure, as a result of my work, was days shy of our daughter's first birthday. They joined me in Costa Rica! My position at the time was with Polymer Solutions and we had a major presence at a specialized trade show in San José, Costa Rica. I had some work to do, but my husband and daughter were able to hang out while I took care of business and then we were able to explore Costa Rica together.

The people we met were so kindhearted and as soon as they learned her birthday was quickly approaching, they enjoyed spoiling her with gifts and sweets. She enjoyed her first bite of cake while in Costa Rica! A sweet woman named Abby gave her a stuffed turtle that we named Yuca, and we still have the stuffy to this day! Much to my delight we got to visit a coffee plantation and learn more about how this magical bean ends up in my mug each morning. I marvel at the opportunity I was able to share with my husband and little girl as a direct result of my work.

My career also has given my husband and me fun ways to get to know each other in new contexts. He was a critical part of me successfully starting and growing my own business, or should I say *our* business. It was more than him simply being supportive. My husband handled all the nuts and bolts of the company that were areas of weakness for me: benefits administration and payroll. We had to wrestle with business decisions as the start-up grew quicker than we ever imagined. Some conversations were filled with friction as we held different opinions, but as we worked through the challenges we grew as a couple.

These are two quick examples of how my work has enhanced my homelife and invited rich experiences for my family.

What about you? How can you pull back and see your work not as a burden that takes away from your family but as a way to bring an added dimension of exploration and joy? I'm certain those examples exist. Choosing to see the way that your career contributes to your family, beyond a paycheck, is a powerful way to fight any mom-guilt you may have over working outside the home.

> **Action Item:** Pause right now and write examples of how your career has brought value to your family—beyond your paycheck.

Not only does your job have an opportunity to bless your family but your experiences at home can also bless your workplace. The lessons I've learned through parenting and on the home front have allowed me to bring more meaning and perspective to the workplace. I enter in with more empathy and understanding as to how our lives outside of working hours dramatically impact how we show up to complete our jobs. I have seen myself grow in my ability to both be gracious and understanding, while also leading with more confidence and wisdom.

I'm a leader, and nothing makes me feel more satisfied than having the opportunity to mentor other leaders. While by no means do I "mother" the people I work with, I find that I can draw parallels to the way I listen and encourage my kids and the way I listen and encourage my colleagues. Both roles have elements of mentorship. Being a leader means having a front row seat to the growth and development of others, just like motherhood. I'm also able to be a wayfinder of sorts to the young women who are wondering the same questions I once did, "Can I have a career and still be a good mom?"

As women, we need to create safe spaces where we can be vulnerable about these struggles. Spaces where we can honestly acknowledge motherhood is the best and simultaneously can be the most exhausting gift. Spaces where we can admit when we feel like we are failing miserably but then receive encouragement as we are reminded that we are exactly what our family needs and that perfection has no place in parenthood.

Celebrating and supporting women who choose to work outside the home in no way takes away or belittles those who choose to work within their home. Each has merit, beauty and impact. I applaud and admire any woman who chooses to embrace the role that makes her come alive and to which she feels God has led her. We all must make the choices that feel true to who we are meant to be and those that will best serve our family.

I do know that when a mom meets her own needs her children are better because of it. For some women, like me, I know that meeting my needs means embracing a vibrant career and being an involved and present mother.

Change is Okay

While motherhood did not end my career it did inspire a major career pivot. At the time we became pregnant I knew that my personal vision for motherhood was mutually exclusive with a career in law enforcement.

It wasn't fear of danger related to police work that prompted the change, it was concern that my work schedule wouldn't allow me to be a present parent. My husband also had an unpredictable work schedule. I wanted one of us to be predictable when it came to our jobs. I felt an aversion to the idea that there would constantly be a force pulling me away from my home life. I wanted to be there at bath time, to tuck my kids in at night, and to be the first face they saw in the morning. I craved a meaningful career that allowed me to fully embrace motherhood.

It was an honor and huge responsibility to serve others as a police officer, often when they were at their worst or in a crisis. To me it wasn't just a job, it was a calling. So, can you imagine my panic when this career path no longer made sense for me? It required a lot of prayer to boldly follow what I felt was a God-given desire to make a big change. I didn't see the big picture or have all the answers when I stepped out in faith to leave law enforcement. But He did. God knows and God sees and therefore, we can trust Him no matter what!

I regularly encounter women who feel stuck working for an organization that hinders their ability to show up fully for their family. Fear often keeps women in places and positions that cause them to compromise their commitment to family. Admittedly, when I was pregnant and knew I wanted out of law enforcement, I struggled to see myself beyond the badge. I was afraid of leaving the known and believing there was something better out there. I felt frustrated and limited by my Criminal Justice degree and wondered whether other employers or industries would have interest in someone like me. I felt trapped.

If there comes a day that you realize your job is forcing you to compromise your commitment to your family, seek input, advice, and truth from those who care most for you. Get their opinions and ideas about what other opportunities might make sense for you. Above all, wash it all in prayer and seek God. Trust that He has marvelous plans for you and He is walking with you, through the workplace struggles.

Life is ever evolving and therefore it's okay if your family and career dynamics have to change alongside the evolution. Don't feel guilty or like you owe the world an apology for changing your mind or learning that what once worked no longer does.

I hope that you will take a deep breath and confidently proceed in the direction that will best meet your needs and the needs of your family. Maybe that's a hard thing to ask of you! Change doesn't happen without consequences. However, when you follow where God leads, even if that means change, you will be blessed for it.

Often when someone is wrestling with the future Jeremiah 29:11 is quickly referenced as a means of encouragement. It states, "For I know the plans I have for you, declares the Lord, plans for welfare and not for evil, to give you a future and a hope."

While there is power, beauty, and truth in this one sentence there is even more Godly wisdom to come. Go on and read the verses that follow: "Then you will call upon me and come and pray to me, and I will hear you. You will seek me and find me, when you seek me with all your heart."[4]

Pray and trust God's ability to do mighty things in your home life and at work. When you feel stress over the future—job security or the career path you are on—go to God first. Turn to Him and His ability to make a way, even if you don't see a way. We are promised that all of our needs will be met. Which is why you can refuse to live in anxiety and concern over your career and your family.

Action Item: Look up Matthew 6:26–34. Spend time reading this beautiful truth that affirms God's promise to always provide for your needs. Allow this scripture to fight any anxiety you may be feeling about the future.

Have To or Get To?

I'm only human and part of that human condition is battling a grumpy attitude about the day-to-day minutia. I'm often focused on the things I'm so annoyed that I "have to" do. Bouncing between a full career and the demands at home often lures me into a grouchy disposition.

4. Jeremiah 29:12-13

By far, my least favorite chore is folding the laundry. It's no big deal to get it into the washing machine and I'm usually pretty reliable about switching it to the dryer. However, after that, all bets are off. Will it sit for 3 days? Maybe just 2. And just how wrinkly will it be by the time I find the motivation to put it on hangers and tuck it away in drawers? The thing I despise only slightly less than folding laundry is ironing laundry. I think you can see how this is all a recipe for domestic meltdown. No doubt about it, keeping up with a household is a lot of work.

Often, I think to myself:

"Ugh, I *have* to put the laundry away."
"I *have* to clean the bathroom."
"I *have* to make dinner."
"I *have* to take the kids to school."
"I *have* to schedule a parent-teacher conference."
"I *have* to _____." How would you fill in that blank?

Where do you find yourself grumbling and annoyed?

As a starting point, let's agree that we are going to take those grumpy thoughts captive, as women of faith. God does not delight in our grumblings or complaints about our mom-life struggles.[5] I'm talking to myself here.

> God does not delight in our grumblings or complaints about our mom-life struggles.

The truth is, I *get* to care for my family. Remember, there was a point in my life where the reality of having children

---

5. 2 Corinthians 10:5

was a struggle and felt impossible. I prayed and prayed for the day I would hold a child in my arms and be blessed with the opportunity to love and care for her and later him. Yes, that means doing laundry and cleaning bathrooms.

I *get* to make us dinner and create food that brings us together, around the same table. Which not only sustains our bodies but also gives us a chance to remember how much better we are together. Some of our most precious family moments are found as we pass the potatoes or enjoy a bite of spaghetti.

I *get* to take my kids to school and have a front row seat as they grow and learn. Seeing them evolve, develop interests, make friends, and navigate challenges is one of the most awe-inspiring experiences. I get to watch it all unfold and cheer for them along the way.

And yes, I *get* to schedule that parent-teacher conference so I can hear all the amazing things they are doing and also step in to advocate for their needs, as it makes sense to do so. This is such a special responsibility.

These are all awesome things I *get* to do because of the blessings of motherhood and marriage. I steal the benefits of God's blessings when I let my bad attitude frame my days. It does not serve me well to walk through the halls of our home grumbling with the laundry basket in my arms. Philippians 2:14 tells us to do everything without complaining. I just checked my Bible and there is no exception noted for when we do the laundry. Therefore, I need to choose my attitude and reflect gratitude.

> I steal the benefits of God's blessings when I let my bad attitude frame my days.

We can apply the same reframing within the context of work outside of the home. The "I have to" can shift into "I get to."

You *get* to lead the team and you get to take on more responsibility. You *get* to be trusted with complicated projects which means you *get* to grow. Your email is flooded with messages because you *get* to be responsible for a lot. You *get* a paycheck because God has blessed you with skills and talents that are marketable and in demand. You *get* to!

As you process the reality of responsibility at work and at home, a perspective of gratitude changes things. It doesn't mean you take on a toxic positivity to your days, but it does mean you submit your thought-life to God and invite Him to transform your way of thinking. Your children are quiet observers of the way you pour into your home, what story are they learning as they watch you?

Remember your coworkers are watching and if you are claiming to be a woman of faith they are considering what that even means. Give them good reasons to be curious about you and how differently you approach your days. Show them that following Jesus changes everything, to include your attitude at work.

A good attitude and a righteous thought life don't mean you're a doormat or that you should allow yourself to be mistreated; I do want to make that clear. You can be full of gratitude but still advocate for fair pay at work. You can be thankful for the blessing of caring for your families but still have expectations that all family members chip in and contribute to the housework. Being grateful and choosing a Christ-like perspective as women still holds space for us to advocate for being treated fairly and with adequate support. I will always advocate for women being brave and bold about boundaries, respect, and equity.

> **Action Item:** Get out a sticky note and simply write the words, "Have to, or get to!?" Now, stick this note somewhere you will regularly see it.

Love and Enjoy Them!

I know that my family knows I love them. That's not enough for me. I want my family to be absolutely certain I enjoy them, too.

I have a goal of covering my family in the kind of delight that energizes them and is life-giving. When my kids look back on their childhood I want them to smile, giggle, and reflect on all the adventures we went on together and all the quirky ways we made the most of our days. When my husband thinks about our marriage, I want him to smile with assurance that I really and truly like doing life alongside him.

While I'm certain that I'm not a perfect wife or mother, I want to get it right when it comes to love-in-action. I don't want to just say it, I want to express it in a way that exclaims, "I delight in who you are!"

My kids feel my delight when I join them in the pool, letting them wrap their arms around my neck as we play "Water Taxi" and dart from one side of the pool to the next. I know my son feels it when I go to tuck him in at night and exclaim "cannonball" while running towards his bed and "jumping" in alongside him. My daughter feels my delight when we lay in bed watching Instagram reels and laugh our faces off or exclaim "awwww" at all the #GoldensofInstagram videos. My husband feels my delight when we steal away for a weekend, just us two. In the quiet and focused time together, I can tell that he's more strikingly aware of how much I enjoy who he is. We reflect on our current reality and dream about our future together.

You can love your family without deeply enjoying them, but where's the fun in that? Wouldn't you rather go through life with a smile on your lips and a giggle waiting to erupt at a moment's notice? Also, consider the powerful combination of love and delight. Don't you think that can be transformative for you and your family?

> Wouldn't you rather go through life with a smile on your lips and a giggle waiting to erupt at a moment's notice?

Having responsibilities outside of the home means that there are others vying for your time and attention, beyond your family. This means you should love your family sincerely and intentionally as God has instructed you to do.[6] Don't give them your second best!

Take the time to ask your family members when they are most sure you enjoy and delight in who they are. That insight will help you be increasingly intentional as you seek to prioritize your relationships with your family members.

I asked my daughter this at one point and it was how I learned being in the pool means so much to her! Without checking in, I may have assumed she would rather be swimming with her friends, but let the record reflect I'm currently still a cool mom.

---

6. 1 Peter 4:8-9

My husband and I have specifically discussed that our weekend trips away are extremely healthy for our marriage and our ability to maintain our commitment to each other. Don't assume you know and don't neglect to ask! Let those you love help shape the way you show up for them.

> Let those you love help shape the way you show up for them.

When you think of those in your life you love most, maybe your children, spouse, or best friend, how do you foster a strong sense of connection? As life evolves and you grow, the connection point may change. Be open to the thing, or things, that will make you both feel seen, heard, valued, and important. Once you find it, *cling to it and nurture it.*

This Matters—You Matter

The way you love your family matters.

If you have fed your family nothing but chicken nuggets all week, you are still wonderful. If your laundry is piled up and the living room is a mess, you are still wonderful. Your worthiness and value is not derived from what you do but rather who you are at your core. God has given you everything you need to love your family well, while working incredibly hard too.

Just so you know, your career matters too.

Whether you are thriving and on top of the world or struggling to get your foot in the door, you are worthy of a career that is meaningful and contributes positively to your life. If this season is especially hard, don't give up! If you find yourself electrified by your ability to contribute in the workplace, relish in how special that is.

It's time for you to release guilt as you live in a family-focused and career-focused way. As you pursue fulfillment in the context of your family and the context of your career, I want you to know—you are worth it and wonderful.

> It's time for you to release guilt as you live in a family-focused and career-focused way.

Brave and Bold Steps Forward

Take time to reflect on how you can bravely and boldly navigate being career-focused and family-focused. Put in the work to push back against guilt and overwhelm. You've got this—I know you do!

1. What has been the most fulfilling aspect of your career? How has your career enriched your family life?
2. How well are you managing the tension between work and family? In what areas do you wrestle with guilt? How can you reframe your guilt with faith perspective?
3. How can you seek God's direction for your career and family, in this season?
4. What are practical steps you can take to more deeply enjoy your family?
5. Take time to write out your five biggest "have to's" and rewrite them as "get to's."

CHAPTER 6

RESPONSIBLE AND JOYFUL

Do you remember the old Toys "R" Us commercials? A sweet little voice would sing, "I don't want to grow up, cause baby if I did, I wouldn't be a Toys "R" Us Kid!" What a catchy jingle! In fact, it was so catchy that I can distinctly remember singing it as a kiddo and then one day, being struck by the reality of growing up. Yikes! I fell apart into a puddle of tears, crying into my mom's lap about the unfair reality of having to grow up. I said I never ever *ever* wanted to grow up.

It does seem that every time I log onto Facebook or scroll my Instagram feed, I'm catching memes and graphics bemoaning the harsh realities of *adulting*. From endless piles of laundry to waking in the middle of the night with kids, the need to show up bright and early to the office and the never-ending home repair projects. It's true, adulting isn't always easy. But, given the choice, would you stay dependent on your parents forever? Likely not.

There are clear benefits to growing up, maturing, and becoming a functioning and contributing member of society; there is undeniable merit to being responsible. There is also immense value in maturing in a way that aligns with God's best for our lives. In doing so, we become more impactful women of faith.[1] It matters that you are responsible!

But not so fast! Choosing fun, living with wonder and taking in each moment is also something to be celebrated. When you pursue joy and embrace a fun-loving spirit you encounter adventure and wonder around every corner. A joyful spirit allows you to fully experience the beauty of creation and the blessings that saturate your life.[2] Life is too serious to be serious all the time—can I get an amen? It's also far too short to waste energy being uptight. God is a straight shooter when it comes to defining our length of time on Earth—it is fleeting.[3]

> When you pursue joy and embrace a fun-loving spirit you encounter adventure and wonder around every corner.

This is yet another area in which so many of us feel tension. We recognize that life expects us to show up and "get it done," but our hearts still long for delight and wonder.

Personally, I love the pairing of responsibility and joy! Although to many they may seem to be qualities that sit in opposition, I find there is a fantastic symbiotic relationship between the two.

1. Ephesians 4:13-16
2. Romans 1:20
3. James 4:14

I've noticed that within my life there are some areas where I'm uncompromisingly serious, but, as a result, these areas yield an abundance of opportunities to embrace good times, create happy memories, and pursue purpose. I also know that I'm a big kid at heart, quirky, and love to laugh. I'm committed to being both responsible and joyful.

Being responsible comes down to the way you steward and manage the resources and gifts that are entrusted to you. This perspective centers on the faith-rooted reasons for living responsibly. Instead of it being about just "doing the right things" it shifts your perspective to taking good care of what God has entrusted to you.

Having a whole lot of fun is a fantastic complement to being serious. When you work diligently to prioritize the areas of your life that matter deeply, you keep yourself in a balanced state that allows joy to flourish. This is also a way that you can lighten up in a world that often feels increasingly dark.

I hope you will join me in the pursuit of a life marked by joy and responsible living!

Rest Is Responsible

Remember, I worry about you.

Right now, I'm worried you don't get adequate rest. I fully accept that this may come across as me trying to "mother" you. Not the intent! I don't mean to nag. I promise, that's not what I'm here for. But I'm strikingly aware of the cultural current that sweeps us away in busyness.

Hustle culture largely prioritizes productivity over our well-being, families, and relationships. It especially prioritizes work over rest. I hope you will become more aware of this pressure to perform and will be brave enough to push back, when needed. Making time and space for rest is responsible, wise, and a great expression of self-care.

When your schedule is overpacked you create conditions in which spontaneous fun is likely not going to happen and worse, you weave stress into your life unnecessarily. Feeling frazzled by racing around to do "all the things" leaves you enjoying none of the things. When you take on too much you rob yourself of joyful experiences and leave no room for rest.

> When your schedule is overpacked you create conditions in which spontaneous fun is likely not going to happen and worse, you weave stress into your life unnecessarily.

To have time for fun you have to manage your schedule and leave moments of pause. Everything you say yes to requires a no to something else. If you say yes to dinner with the girls you are saying no to a quiet night at home with your husband. If you say yes to another meeting you are saying no to productivity time in your office. If you say yes to another playdate you are saying no to an opportunity to engage one-on-one with your child. It's not that either option is inherently good or bad, it's simply that you can't exist in two places at once.

Your value is not rooted in your to-do list. I hope you really heard me when I said that—maybe go read the previous sentence again and again until you start to believe me. While we are at it, let me underscore that your worth is not tied to how many activities you can cram into one 24-hour period. Hustle culture may sound good on social media, but it won't feel good when you're burnt out from trying to push your days right up until the edge of a meltdown.

> Hustle culture may sound good on social media, but it won't feel good when you're burnt out from trying to push your days right up until the edge of a meltdown.

God Himself built rest into our schedules. Remember the sabbath? Remember how we are instructed to keep it Holy?[4] This is affirmation that we are not made to hustle 7 days a week—we were created with limits. We were also given a solution and a model for rest. As Jesus pointed out, taking a Sabbath is not a legalistic weekly ritual but a loving gift.[5] Let's not be too stubborn to take on a Sabbath mentality.

Find time to slip into "Sabbath Mode" in which you are restful and stop the hustle. You can trust God will give you the energy and ideas to accomplish your work the other days of the week. Have faith that you can pause, allow time for rest and still accomplish a sufficient amount of work and activities. Rest really is responsible.

Rest does not have to be boring nothingness. Let's go ahead and dismantle that misconception. You can find rest in nature, as you play with your kids, during a board game night, or while you relax on the couch. It simply means you are intentionally taking a break from productivity.

You need adequate sleep every night and days off from work. Don't believe me? Go read Genesis and take a look at what God modeled. He finished making all of creation and

4. Exodus 34:21
5. Mark 2:27-28

paused to rest on the 7th day. When God rested, He declared that it was Holy.[6] This is something for us all to internalize and reflect upon as we fight back against busyness.

Jesus modeled this measured way of living, too. He did not "hustle" His way to the cross. His ministry unfolded through the pages of the gospel with intent—and with rest. He enjoyed meals with friends. He made time to connect with people. Jesus went off to quiet places to pray. He did not go from preaching one sermon to the next, to the next, without a break in between. Since we don't see hustle culture modeled anywhere in scripture, I feel confident suggesting that you abandon the practice and embrace a more measured way of living, too. Go enjoy a meal with your bestie. Take time to slowly sip your coffee and watch the sun rise. Run around outside like a child and if you are feeling especially joyful, do a cartwheel!

If you are a people pleaser then everything I've just asked you to do may feel incredibly difficult. It can be hard to rest when you know there are many people vying for your time and benefitting from your productivity. This is made near-impossible when your only reason for saying no is because you want time to have fun. As you wrestle you may reason that you can surely send just one more email. Or, maybe just one more extracurricular for your kids wouldn't be so bad.

Be brave! Be bold! Manage your time in a way that allows you to breathe in goodness and holds space for joyful expressions. Remember that you are living as a woman of faith when you insist that rest is something you need in your life.

---

6. Genesis 2:2-3

Action Item: Take out your calendar and honestly look at your schedule. Have you booked yourself so full that you are lacking space for fun or rest? Consider what time boundaries you can establish moving forward to live in a more measured way.

Prioritize People

When thinking about the idea of responsibility I can't help but think of being a good steward. When talking about the word "steward" our minds often default to dollar bills. We think about the responsibility we have to manage money and funds. I think we forget that in God's economy, there is something held in much higher esteem than money: people.

People are of the utmost importance to God. He set them apart from the rest of creation in the earliest days of the world. In one of the sweetest demonstrations of how He feels about us, God described the first five days of His creation as "good," but then on the sixth day He made man and commented it was "very good."[7] *That* says something significant about where people fall in His hierarchy of creation!

Recognizing How God loves people means that the way you love others matters. This is why it's so important you are responsible in the way you invest in, nurture, and protect relationships. You cannot be so dedicated to productivity and your schedule that you fail to remain dedicated to people.

While leading and growing Blue Mobius Marketing, my marketing agency, I never had long-term sales projections or financial growth goals. I lived by the mantra, "take care of

---

7. Genesis 1:31

people and the rest will take care of itself." That was a way to express my faith-rooted conviction within the workplace. In addition to honoring God, it worked beautifully well for my business. The marketing agency was strategically acquired only 18-months after launch.

My business mantra felt easy most of the time, but there were situations in which I was really challenged to apply it. The most poignant example was when I cut ties with our largest client because of how they were treating our team. There was an explosive situation amongst their employees that left my team feeling unsafe emotionally and physically. When I spoke with their CEO there was no ownership or path forward, it was minimizing and denial. As a result, I knew what I had to do. I politely ended the relationship in a way that was above reproach and with kindness. I needed my team to know that they were more valuable than the contract and I would do everything in my power to protect their emotional and physical well-being. I had to take care of people.

That meant I took a short-term financial loss. Yes, that stung and made me sweat (a lot), but I trusted that God would continue to provide. I was completely right and leaning into my faith did not disappoint. We had one month of financial struggle, but it was eclipsed by the financial strength we experienced every other month to come.

We need to put first things first as we journey through life. Within our careers and home lives we can't let our priorities get out of whack because of ambitious goals or weighty to-do lists. Jesus spelled out what should be our priorities, in response to being asked directly what the most important commandment is. Jesus answered:

You shall love the Lord your God with all your heart and
with all your soul and with all your mind. This is the great
and first commandment. And a second is like it: You shall
love your neighbor as yourself. On these two commandments depend all the Law and the Prophets.[8]

Jesus told us what is most important: God and people.
Make sure you are always holding space for this truth.

What does it look like to prioritize people and to be a good
steward of relationships? It could mean pausing the project
you are working on to sit and listen to a coworker who is
navigating a grief journey. It means putting your laptop away
to take a break and attend a birthday luncheon for your colleague. In your home life, it means putting down the vacuum
to play Candyland with your child. It can also mean saying
"yes" to coffee with a friend, even though you've already had
coffee and you have a lot of things to get done. Make prioritizing people part of your personal ministry.

Owning Your Faith

Being responsible means assuming a sense of ownership for
something. You realize you are accountable and "on the hook"
for that thing. When reflecting on the various things we are
responsible for, and the things we should nurture, there is
something at the very top of that list. We just spent time
centering ourselves on the commandment that Jesus defined
as the second most important commandment: loving others
as ourselves. Do you remember what came right before that

8. Matthew 22:36-40

in Matthew 22:37–38? Jesus said, "You shall love the Lord your God with all your heart and with all your soul and with all your mind. This is the great and first commandment."

Of all the things we are responsible for, our faith is at the top of the list.

I love how in scripture it speaks to our hearts, souls, and mind. This helps give a framework for what it looks like to love God deeply. It's not just about a warm fuzzy feeling, it's also about the way our minds learn and grow. It's also not just head knowledge. Our love for God needs to align our head

> Our love for God needs to align our head with our heart as truth takes root in the depths of our souls.

with our heart as truth takes root in the depths of our souls. Our faith should define every aspect of who we are.

Taking responsibility for your faith means that you realize you are accountable to God directly. You can't leave your faith formation in the hands of your parents, pastor, best friend, or husband. All of these people can play a supporting role and guide you, but they cannot let you off the hook. Nor should you want to be off the hook! It's awe-inspiring that the God of the Universe wants to know you intimately and personally.

Owning your faith means worshiping God as you seek to love Him with all your heart. It also means entering into reflective states of prayer and confession as you seek to love Him with all your soul. It's also taking care to learn more about God as you seek to love Him with all your mind.

Often the ways of the world are often very inconsistent with a life rooted in a faith foundation.[9] Don't just go with

---

9. Romans 12:2

the flow and allow yourself to be swept up in cultural currents. Through scripture, prayer, and worship you can begin to grab onto your faith with both hands.

Cartwheeling Christian

I've always been deeply silly and quirky on the inside, but I have found that the stronger my faith, the less serious I take myself. As my faith increases, so does my joy. I may be noticing a few gray hairs here and there, but my soul feels

> As my faith increases, so does my joy.

younger and spryer than ever. Isn't that a fun reality? Being confident that my identity is rooted in Jesus gives me the freedom to live with abandon, not bound by concerns over how I sound or what I look like. That is one of the most wonderful ways that our faith can transform us; we can shed our insecurities as we mature and develop in this critical aspect of who we are.

Do you know that feeling of excited-overwhelm when you realize the majesty of God? I often experience it on a sandy beach when I look out to the horizon and see the power of the waves. I sense it when I step outside after a fresh snow and the hush surrounds me. I also feel it when I walk into a grassy field and marvel at the green vibrancy that speaks to a loving Creator. Nature does declare God's majesty and I feel so wonderfully overwhelmed when I get to experience it![10] I feel moved toward wonder and I just can't help myself; I have to do a cartwheel.

I'm indeed a cartwheeling Christian. I'm a woman who feels deep joy in the Lord. I like to think of those cartwheels

10. Romans 1:20

as a sweet and silly expression of my faith that moves me. I also like to imagine a heavenly smirk on His face while I turn in circles. Afterall, childlike faith is applauded and what's more childlike than a cartwheel?[11] When you feel the spirit of God move you into a place of wonder and awe, I hope you will act on it. My cartwheels aren't pretty—at all—but I know in His eyes they are perfect.

I sincerely hope you will nurture your childlike faith and invite more joy to take up residence in your heart. And hey, if it prompts you to do a cartwheel too, all the better!

My silly antics don't stop with cartwheels! Would you believe that I actually giggled out loud as I wrote this chapter? I did. I may be the biggest kid that I know. I have a Peter Pan commitment to never grow up and I love any opportunity I can take to be lighthearted and laugh!

One of the best "inner child" things I've done in my adult years is to go to Disney World *without* my kids. Can you believe I would dare do such a thing? Initially, I fought guilt that I was going to one of the happiest, most magical, and child-centered places on Earth without my kids. Once that initial wave of guilt had come and gone, my inner child was delighted and eager for the experience.

On this trip I was traveling to meet up with my sister, her husband and my nephew who I had never met before. The trip was all kinds of magic! My parents came too, which meant they could keep the baby while us big kids went off to explore and conquer Disney.

There I was, standing in the shade at Animal Kingdom, taking a break from all the fun and activity. I was sipping

---

11. Matthew 18:3

an iced Americano from Starbucks because, well, *coffee*. As I stood there, a cast member (aka, a Disney employee) approached our group and asked if we wanted to be in a celebratory parade that would move across Animal Kingdom.

At first, I hesitated, as did everyone in my family. This would mean uninhibited engagement and putting myself out there for all the other Disney guests to observe, see, and potentially judge. With those hesitations in mind, I weighed the pros and cons and realized this was my one shot. It was my moment. Although initially no one else in my family was willing to join I was aware I'd never again be in that place, at that time, able to dance my heart out in a Disney parade. When Disney asks you to join a dance party, *you don't say no!*

Once my internal debate was firmly settled, I jumped right in and knew it was time to give it my all. At the last minute, and to my delight, my dad joined me. For the record, he joined me but most assuredly did not *really* want to go. However, I'm confident he doesn't regret his decision as he looks back at it.

They led us back to an area where the Disney cast members in the parade were gathering. The men and women were adorned in elaborate costumes and were breathtakingly beautiful. I immediately felt underdressed in my yoga pants and Little Mermaid tank, but I didn't let that stop me! I joined a handful of other park guests and did my best to make Mickey proud with my moves. I let go, swirled my streamers, and felt the music against the vibrant backdrop of the Animal Kingdom.

The parade concluded in a big courtyard and a live band was waiting for us. I was amazed at how many people joined us in the uninhibited dance. We didn't care who was or wasn't watching, we just felt the music and let ourselves go. I felt unstoppable, I felt alive.

Disney brought out my inner child in ways that were so refreshing. It's amazing how stepping back into simpler times has a way of refocusing us and mitigating the stresses of adulthood that can all too easily weigh us down. I wonder if you are willing to say yes to opportunities to let go and embrace your silly self? Are you able to not take yourself too seriously?

It doesn't take going to Disney World to immerse yourself in childlike joy. It can be as simple as playing a game of pretend with a child, going to the local arcade with a friend, or trying something new for the first time. I so badly want you to let go and not worry who is watching. Who cares if they have something to say? They'll be saying it from the sidelines as you experience life for all its vibrancy.

Pause right now and think back to the last time you felt uninhibited joy! Did you dance in the rain? Did you laugh until you were gasping for breath? Was it a moment that took your breath away? I want you to sit with it and consider the experience. That is what I'm asking you to seek out again, and again. Moments that make you pull back in wonder at who you were made to be and the world you were given to experience.

> Who cares if they have something to say? They'll be saying it from the sidelines as you experience life for all its vibrancy.

When was the last time you tried something for the first time? Think about how special a "first" can be! One of the best parts of being a parent is watching my children take in new experiences for the first time. When they were babies it was as simple as their first solid food. It was so fun and funny to watch them delight over peaches and pears while also giggling as their button noses scrunched up in response to peas. We laughed and clapped together as the culinary experience of first foods unfolded.

As they have grown, there have been so many wonderful opportunities to enjoy a front row seat to so many firsts: their first snow, first time swimming, first glimpse at the ocean, first Christmas. Wow, what wonder!

I encourage you to create a goal of trying something new at least every three months. Make it a bite sized and measurable goal that you will use to hold yourself accountable. It can be as simple or as complex as your time and budget allows. Maybe you go to a trampoline park or indoor rock-climbing wall. If you are in the mood for a more subdued experience, an art class could be a way to comfortably push you towards a fun new pursuit. It could even be a new restaurant or style of cuisine. It must be new!

Each day has infinite opportunities for the "new," but somehow we fall into rhythms and routines that seem to be mutually exclusive with adventure, exploration, and the pursuit of "firsts." I wonder if it frustrates God that we tend to become overly responsible as adults and, as a result, we fail to approach His blessings with amazement. Again, we can't forget that childlike faith is celebrated.

> I wonder if it frustrates God that we tend to become overly responsible as adults and, as a result, we fail to approach His blessings with amazement.

Take on everyday experiences with fresh eyes for creative input. Instead of just having lunch, consider using teacups for your drink and all of a sudden, your lunch just transformed into a tea party! That tiny touch will take you from everyday ho-hum to delightful and immersive! Maybe in July you bring out your snowman mug, fill it with hot chocolate and turn on Christmas carols to celebrate Christmas in July. Bonus points if you watch *How the Grinch Stole Christmas*, which I am certain is the best Christmas movie of all time!

> It's so much more fun when your joy bubbles up from within and transforms the ordinary into extraordinary!

It's so much more fun when your joy bubbles up from within and transforms the ordinary into extraordinary!

Laugh Until Your Stomach Hurts

Despite your best efforts to let loose and have fun, there are situations and seasons in life that you just can't seem to catch a break. Times in which life feels punishingly hard and fun feels foreign. Although we know as women of faith we are expected to find joy regardless of our circumstances, sometimes that feels out of the question.[12]

While the circumstances you are facing may be impossible to change, your ability to laugh can help lighten the load. Can you laugh without fear of the future?[13] My mom seems to have mastered that ability!

My mom is one of the people in my life who keeps me from taking myself too seriously. I talk to her once a day, sometimes

---

12. 1 Thessalonians 5:16-18
13. Proverbs 31:25

> While the circumstances you are facing may be impossible to change, your ability to laugh can help lighten the load. Can you laugh without fear of the future?

more. She is ever present and strong and steady. She's also guaranteed to laugh really hard at my stories—even the ones that aren't supposed to be funny.

Although sometimes I find her laughter to be untimely, I know that she's able to loosen me up and help me let go. It's hard to stay crabby when the person on the other end of the phone is cackling. Before I know it, she has reframed some aspect of my frustration or anger into something worth giggling about. Do you have a friend like that? If so, I suggest you make a plan to call her more often—she's one to hold onto!

When I was a patrol officer on midnight shift, I called my mom on my commute home every single morning. I had a 30-minute drive and our conversation not only kept my eyes open but helped me process all that had transpired the night before. As a police officer I experienced a mixture of strange, scary and intriguing things. I'll never forget one of my calls to her on my drive home, after a really intense night at work. I had gotten into my first foot pursuit.

The radio call had been dispatched as a "screams for help" call within a trailer park. I arrived on scene at the exact same time as one of my favorite coworkers and together we confronted the situation. Very long story short: It was a domestic violence situation, and the aggressor ultimately went to jail.[14]

---

14. If you are in a Domestic Violence situation, please get help: 1-800-799-7233 (National Hotline)

The call itself was not funny at all. However, one aspect of the call was beyond ridiculous. The suspect was naked. *Yes, naked.*

As we got on scene the birthday-suit-bandit managed to slip out of the trailer and into the wooded area of the trailer park. Of course, he ultimately emerged from the portion of the perimeter I was watching—he literally came streaking by my post.

As I recounted this story to my mom, in lots of colorful details, I made sure she knew this really was a dangerous, stressful, and difficult situation. I specifically told her it wasn't funny. However, when I got to the part about chasing a naked suspect, she came undone. She had been well behaved long enough and could no longer hold back the flood gate of laughter. She cackled and howled on the phone, and I just sat still, waiting for her to finish. It took quite a while.

Yeah, she was right, it was pretty ridiculous.

Everyone went home safely, and I had plenty of support from my fellow officers, I wasn't even the one that had to tackle the guy or cuff him (#BLESSED). It really was stressful at first, but since everyone went home safe that night (and the naked guy got pants) my mom was right—it was worth laughing about! So, I joined her in snorting laughter at the hilarity of what happened.

My mom offers such a great juxtaposition to the serious roles I have consistently found myself occupying in life. Through her laughter and lighthearted perspective, she gives me the freedom to relax and release the weight of the world. Laughter lightens me up.

I hope you will allow laughter to offset the heavy in your day. If you can see the silly side, please do! "A joyful heart is good medicine"—so go ahead and giggle.[15] It may be that your inclination is toward more of a serious disposition and laughter doesn't come easy for you. If this is the case, surround yourself with people who can help you lighten up. My mom does this for me and I know that she offers comic relief to situations I would otherwise allow myself to wallow in.

> While you can't control the wild things that may come your way, you can fight to control your response. Seek opportunities to lean into laughter and lighten up.

While you can't control the wild things that may come your way, you can fight to control your response. Seek opportunities to lean into laughter and lighten up.

Quirky and Wonderfully Made

I'm quirky. Are you?

I'm pretty sure we all are, if we really start peeling back the layers and shared honestly about the little details that make us who we are. If we would be brave enough to share our little odd ways and chuckle together, I think our days would be more fun and sillier.

I'll go first. I like my sandwiches cut in two rectangles. I don't like being barefoot. I could eat pizza all day every day. I'm obsessed with colorful Paper Mate flair tip pens. I like doing impressions of people and making up funny voices. I've never watched *Star Wars*—ever (which may be dangerous to put in writing!). I really don't like skiing, rollerblading, or ice skating—basically any activity in which I can't control my own

---

15. Proverbs 17:22

two feet. If I start reading a book I feel compelled to finish it, no matter how much I dislike the book. Oh, and I much prefer drinking room temperature water to ice cold water.

Action Item: Your turn! What are your quirky little details? How has God knit you together in a way that is wonderful and even a little silly? Go ahead, write out your list! While you do, don't forget to smile about how wonderfully unique you are.

Part of feeling the freedom to live joyfully is you coming to terms with who you are. Self-awareness of who God made you to be, and delighting in that reality, makes it easier to live freely.

Letting yourself off the hook for the aspects you think might be weird or odd is a gift you can experience when your identity is defined by God. Please give yourself that gift today! Recognizing you are fearfully and wonderfully made will also help you embrace your quirks.[16]

Remember, God knows everything about you from the number of hairs on your head to the days you will live on this Earth.[17] He won't be surprised by your preference for writing in only colorful ink or your love for animated movies. It won't shock Him to see you have a fascination for historical trivia or an aversion to seafood. I imagine all those little fun details make Him smile as He thinks, "Yep, I made her!"

Your ability to pursue joyful living reflects the impact of faith on your life! As Christians, we are reminded many times to be joyful in all things. Joy is a way to let the

16. Psalm 139:14
17. Luke 12:7

> Joy is a way to let the transformational power of your faith shine brightly through you.

transformational power of your faith shine brightly through you. If you are grumpy and overly serious all the time people may not realize a love relationship with Jesus changes everything. Let your light shine bright so it encourages others to consider what faith could do for them, too.[18]

Beyond the personal benefits of living into your uniqueness, it also blesses others! You should bring your best self into your relationships and community. In doing so, you will contribute in the most impactful way possible. Each of us has a different way of showing up and gifts we can contribute to the greater good.[19] Playing small serves nobody well. We need the true you, including all your quirks, to show up!

Embrace the days that God has blessed you with—laughing, loving, and soaking up every bit of goodness. Also, take care of the important things so that you have the freedom to enjoy God's best for you.

Brave and Bold Steps Forward

I hope you will bravely and boldly live a life that is both responsible and joyful! Use these prompts as a way to examine your heart and consider your next steps.

1. In honest reflection, do you feel your life is one truly marked by joy regardless of the circumstances? Is it something others would describe as contagious?

---

18. Matthew 5:15-16
19. Romans 12:4-5

2. If you had to give yourself a letter-grade for how well you are prioritizing people, what would that grade be? Elaborate on your reasoning and realizations.

3. What is one new thing you can try in the next month? Go ahead and put it on your schedule—make it happen!

4. What does rest look like for you these days? How can you take on a Sabbath-mindset as you consider being both responsible and joyful?

5. Consider all your quirks and determine which one is your favorite. How does it set you apart from others? How does it invite vibrancy into your days?

CHAPTER 7

LOVELY AND FIERCE

One of the highest compliments I can give another woman is to describe her as lovely. To me, that word has a smooth texture and I appreciate how it feels when I say it. The word is comprehensive and multidimensional—so much more than being beautiful or attractive. Woven into that one word I see poise and grace paired with a pleasing presence. Simply lovely.

Another one of the highest compliments can I give another woman is to describe her as fierce. Oh, that word! I feel my top teeth on my bottom lip as the first syllable emerges—it feels aggressive. My eyebrows raise up as I utter it, emphasizing the punch of what this word means. To describe a woman as fierce is honoring her fighter spirit. When I think of the word fierce, I imagine a warrior who is ready to take action if needed but who also has the wisdom to wait for the right time and the right battle.

If you put those two words together, lovely and fierce, you are describing my favorite kind of person. I love to surround myself with women who have poise and polish but also carry a fighter's spirit with them, everywhere they go.

Do you know someone like this? I do.

Beautiful Warrior

My friend, colleague, sister-in-Christ, and boss, Joy Reyes, is the embodiment of lovely and fierce. People often ask how I came to know New Hope Girls and entered into friendship with Joy and her family. It was an "only God" kind of introduction. Many years ago she and I had a divine appointment over coffee at Starbucks.

That divine appointment happened through a local business connection who later became a sweet friend. Chris had shared about her experiences within the Dominican Republic and brought up New Hope Girls in the process. My interest piqued and I felt beckoned into the story—eager for every detail.

A couple weeks later Joy happened to be in my hometown, visiting Chris. Ever the connector and relationship builder, Chris felt we needed to meet in person. The meeting was short and intense. Joy told me all about New Hope Girls and that was my inaugural set of tears I cried over New Hope and the story the organization carries.

As she told me about her willingness to "give it all up" and move to a developing country, I sat in awe. At that point in my life, I didn't have a faith that completely understood Joy's level of commitment and fight. That could be what made me all the more curious and amazed by how she and her family choose to live. They are all-in for the Lord and His call on their life.

Equally amazing to me was how this beautiful woman, with a poetic rhythm to her voice, was the same woman who just told me she personally rescued an 8-year-old girl from a brothel. One day, when she realized the horrors happening, she walked in, and the little girl reached out for her. Hand in hand, they left that pit of darkness and walked out into the light.

Although the rescue methods have changed over the years, Joy still goes to every hard place needed—figuratively and literally—to advocate for these precious girls. She goes into courts and meets with political and government officials to fight. She sits with girls in crisis and helps them learn how to regulate, when the trauma of their past threatens to overwhelm. She does not shy away from the tough stuff! She is fierce.

Joy also has a great sense of style and taste. She's responsible for selecting each one of our luxurious fabrics that later are turned into our artisan-made bags. She has an eye! Her sense of fashion is on point and can pivot from a trendy and funky vibe to feminine and delicate. But then, she'll be the first to throw on oversized sweats and a hoodie to sit around a fire and just relax. She doesn't always have to be "on," she's also so comfortable being casual. She is lovely.

When I think of Micah 6:8 (NIV), "... And what does the Lord require of you? To act justly and to love mercy and to walk humbly with your God. Act justly and to love mercy and to walk humbly with God" I think of Joy. She seeks to make change and has a way of stifling fears and insecurities because she knows the work she has been called to is supremely important. Joy operates from a place of conviction that all the fights she's fighting are ultimately the Lord's and she has merely been given an invitation to be faithful in her calling. Wow, she's such an encouragement to me in how she lives her life in service to others and in alignment with her faith.

Joy is so certain of who she is that she radiates beauty from within—the kind of beauty that comes from an identity found in Christ. She also is so sure of who she is that she can shut down fear and insecurity to do hard things and go to hard places. My dear friend is the epitome of both lovely and fierce. She has been a tremendous encouragement to me as I seek to act justly, love mercy and walk humbly with God.

Spend time considering the women you admire deeply. Allow yourself to be inspired by the ways that they are lovely and fierce. It's special to have role models in our lives that encourage us to be stronger women of faith, simply by the way they live. Open your eyes wide to the lovely and fierce women that impact you.

Kicking in Doors

Sometimes when I speak with a group of people who are leaning in, focused, and engaged, I say things that are a bit surprising. Actually, this happens so often I wonder why I even surprise myself anymore, ha! I get hyped up as I get going in front of the room. The energy from the crowd fuels me and encourages my antics forward. My mind starts doing gymnastics with all the colorful ways I can tell stories or prove points. Sometimes the momentum carries me in such a way that before I know it, I've said something that catches me off guard.

One memorable demonstration of this Caitlyn-Speaking-Phenomenon was when I was presenting to a really smart group of students at Virginia Tech. The purpose of the talk was to speak about my career trajectory and lessons learned along the way. The goal was to provide actionable insight as they pursue their academic and career goals.

I explained the drivers behind my first career in Law Enforcement. I shared that for as long as I could remember I wanted to pursue justice and help the vulnerable. I felt a drive to advocate for those who didn't have a voice or had been victimized. I've never been able to tolerate seeing others mistreated, so to me the most logical career move was to be a police officer. I told that group of students that I wanted to "kick in doors."

I literally said those words: kick in doors.

What in the world?! I did not start my career in law enforcement with a desire to splinter wood and make a grand entrance. That's not what I meant. Truth be told, in my five years of law enforcement I never personally kicked in a single door. However, to this day I love what that illustration represents. I believe that is why those words still come to mind and out of my mouth. In stating "I wanted to kick in doors" I meant that I wanted to be fearless in my pursuit of justice and risk it all to help those who genuinely needed me. That nothing would dissuade me from my mission.

But what was more curious than my original word choice was how those words came full circle in my presentation.

After taking the class through my full career story I landed on my current reality: my beautiful opportunity to support New Hope Girls with social entrepreneurship. Before I realized what was happening those words came out of my mouth again, "I'm kicking in doors again."

Whoa. Those are strong words; they are fighting words. And that is exactly the point.

Human trafficking, exploitation and abuse are so horrifically ugly. Our average age at intake is 10 years old. However, we have intercepted infants and regularly welcome girls as young as four. This darkness of exploitation preys on the vulnerable, damages identities, and replaces truth with lies. It attacks with layers and layers of trauma. So yes, I fight. *I kick in doors.*

In this current season, the doors I "kick in" are still not literally wood. I kick in doors with social entrepreneurship. I use the skills, talents, and experiences I've accumulated over my career to advance the work of New Hope Girls. As I do my job well, the workshop component of the organization grows. As we grow, more women are employed in a safe way that allows them to provide for their family with dignity and honor. I'm in the business of doing my part so that cycles can be broken and empowerment can be ushered in. I'm just one person—but I'm one determined person who is part of a team of warriors.

As you know, I've joined a team of "door kickers" down in the Dominican Republic. No, they are not literally kicking in doors either. Remember, those early days of rescue have evolved, but figurative doors are still splintering and shattering as they love and support girls coming from the darkest of places. Each of us, from our cook to our artisans, from our therapists to our founder and leadership team, is fighting for hope and healing. We are fierce in our resolve and hold nothing back, giving our all to see just one more rescued. Just one more brought into our homes of light and peace. Just one more we can hold and speak truth over—*you were created for more.*

While my words during that speaking engagement may have initially surprised me, they make so much sense now. I'm fueled by a soul-level conviction that these women and girls are worth more. I willingly and proudly own that I'm fierce.

Do You Want to Kick in Doors?

I love how many of us have heart-level issues that we care deeply about. There is much darkness in our world and God has invited us to be the salt of the Earth and a marvelous light.[1] He is clear about our role as it relates to fighting back and the battles that rage, "Beloved, never avenge yourselves, but leave it to the wrath of God, for it is written, 'Vengeance is mine, I will repay, says the Lord.'"[2]

> There is much darkness in our world and God has invited us to be the salt of the Earth and a marvelous light.

Being fierce isn't about being a vigilante or seeking a fight. It's not about walking around fueled by anger or hatred. It's about recognizing that burning in your belly when you encounter an issue that you know goes against God's design for our world. It could be awareness of abuse or exploitation. Your heart issues may relate to the Foster Care system or international adoption. Or perhaps, you care deeply about the beauty of our Earth and God's creation. Spend time considering what stirs your soul and then ask yourself, what are you going to do about it? Is God asking you to kick in a proverbial door?

1. Matthew 5:13-16
2. Romans 12:19

James 1:27 reminds us, "Religion that pure and undefiled before God the Father is this: to visit orphans and widows in their affliction." You have a responsibility to others and to reflect the love of Jesus in this hurting and broken world. Think about the powerful ministry of Jesus! He went into hard places to love others well. He got up close and personal with societal outcasts—prostitutes, lepers, people with physical afflictions. Jesus looked them in the eyes and offered relief and love. He was fierce in His resolve to use His life to be the most brilliant and beautiful light this world has ever seen. Will you follow in those fierce footsteps?

You can find your role and area of impact. Share your time, talent, and treasure in a way that honors your desire to be a light. Use your experiences and skills to fill in a service gap. Give generously to support those who are serving on the front lines. Buy products from brands that are on the front lines of the issues God has placed on your heart. There are vulnerable, hurting, and at-risk people who are waiting for doors to be kicked open for them. Find your corner and fiercely—and righteously—fight!

What Beauty Do You Seek?

As much as I love to be fierce and enjoy the feeling of standing strong, I also enjoy the softer and sweeter side of who I get to be. I love to be a nurturer and want to be the kind of woman that is graceful, gracious, and kind.

It makes me so happy when my kids invite me on the couch to simply snuggle—my presence and affection is enough for them. I love when we invite guests into our home and can practice hospitality and make them feel welcome and wanted.

I really enjoy being friendly to others, making them feel seen and celebrated, because I know that they are seen and celebrated by God. It feels good to be the kind of person that is considerate, thoughtful, and empathetic. A lovely person.

It matters to me that I reflect an internal beauty that comes from the faith foundation of who I am. I want to be a 1 Corinthians 13:4–7 kind of lovely.

> Love is patient and kind; love does not envy or boast; it is not arrogant or rude. It does not insist on its own way; it is not irritable or resentful; it does not rejoice at wrongdoing, but rejoices with the truth. Love bears all things, believes all things, hopes all things, endures all things.

I want to be patient and kind. I don't want to envy, boast or be arrogant. I want to honor others and be selfless, slow to anger. I want to let go of wrongs—never delighting in evil but rejoicing in truth. I want to trust, hope and persevere—always.

Action Item: Write out 1 Corinthians 13:4–7 replacing each use of the word "love" with Jesus. Allow yourself to be amazed and inspired by the realization that He is perfect love and our best example for lovely living.

And you? What type of loveliness are you striving for? What type of beauty do you seek most in this world? Are you after the filter-perfect beauty found on Instagram or the red-carpet-ready glamor found in the pages of magazines?

Loveliness is in the Lord. That is where eternal beauty comes from and that is what will set you apart in a crowd of people: the glow of walking with your Father intimately, each and every day. The most beautiful women I know are these types of women.

> Loveliness is in the Lord. That is where eternal beauty comes from and that is what will set you apart in a crowd of people

I encourage you to commit to practicing the necessary soul-care, not just self-care, that will begin to makeover your heart into an increasingly lovely version of yourself. One of the ways that I do this is by seeking to know God's character more and more. Make it all about Him and who He is. In the process, He will give you a glorious makeover. He will transform the way you think, believe, and behave. The way you see yourself in light of His glory will also be powerfully reframing.

I urge you to consider how you are pursuing faith perspective in your daily life. Become incredibly curious about who God is and how deeply He loves you. This will be the loveliest work you could ever do!

Our External Lovely

You and I can't deny that we are situated in a world that also puts immense pressure on women to possess external, worldly beauty. This pressure can lead to a never-ending pursuit of the perfect skin, body, hair, nails, eyelashes, wardrobe—and more. We buy all the skin care products, pay for manicures, invest in wardrobe refreshes, and at times even undergo cosmetic procedures.

As a woman of faith, with confidence in where your true inner beauty lies, you must carefully and reasonably approach issues of self-esteem, external beauty, and self-care. There's no denying that these things matter on some level, but you can't allow yourself to be so consumed by your physical appearance that you lose sight of your innate, internal, and eternal value.

> You can't allow yourself to be so consumed by your physical appearance that you lose sight of your innate, internal, and eternal value.

Fighting to feel attractive is something that is a shared struggle. There may be a woman here or there that has mastered the art of being consistently comfortable in her own skin, but, if I had to guess, that has taken work. It's also a journey in and of itself because, as life changes, our bodies change, and our feelings about how we look also change.

Over the course of my life my body has ebbed in flow, my hair cuts have as well. I went through this fantastic, multi-year period of having blunt bangs. Even as I write this, I miss those fantastic bangs! I rocked them while I had them and then later moved on to the more side swept look.

Back in my police officer days my sense of style and fashion were seriously limited. We had rules around nail polish and hair, it had to be pulled up and off my collar or short enough it didn't hit my collar. I often went to work feeling plain and my wardrobe was drab. Wearing a patrol uniform every day meant that I did not invest much in nice clothes. For court appearances, I had a black suit and white button up I'd wear occasionally. I was seriously simple. However, I distinctly remember a fellow female officer turning to me and saying, "you are too girly."

Funny, I look back and remember being light on makeup (a little neutral eyeshadow and mascara) and either had my hair cut short enough that it didn't hit my collar (super cute, inverted bob) or had it up in a ponytail or bun. My nails were never painted. I didn't wear ornate jewelry or have lash extensions. I also had the extra bulk of a bulletproof vest. I explain all this to say that, by my standards, I was showing up "plain," but by others' standards I was showing up "too girly." Do you see the issue here?

You can't let other people define what it means for you to feel comfortable with your appearance. You'll waste a lot of time and effort attempting to achieve that subjective end goal. Instead, show up in a way that feels true to who you are and how you want to be perceived. It matters most that you are at peace with your appearance and work to feel lovely in your own skin. You can be strikingly lovely at any size, shape, or age.

I know that I also feel the most comfortable in my own skin when I'm putting in the work to be healthy. I love food (a lot!) but know that overindul-

> It matters most that you are at peace with your appearance and work to feel lovely in your own skin. You can be strikingly lovely at any size, shape, or age.

gence leads me feeling sluggish physically. It has taken time and effort to learn how to fuel my body in a way that tastes good, feels good and is long term sustainable.

I'm also emotionally healthiest when I'm regularly running and getting outdoors for exercise and fresh air. Exercise is as much about my mental well-being as my physical self. I find that as I move my body, my mind relaxes, and I finish exercising much more balanced. With my decades of living, I have a much better sense of what it takes to feel lovely inside and out.

How are you taking care of your body and appearance? Are you over emphasizing the external at the cost of the more important internal work? Are you allowing yourself to show up confidently in a way that feels true to you? How about your nutrition—are you considering how the food choices you make can energize you and sustain you?

Have you stopped to consider that your body is on loan to you? An earthly vessel that carries an eternal soul?[3] God gave it to you so you can be a good steward while you are living on this side of heaven. We must care for ourselves in a way that expresses gratitude for the body we have been given—even if we do experience aches, pains, and afflictions of humanity.

I love reframing exercise in that context! It's so much more special to think about running as a way to worship or lifting weights as an act of gratitude. If you go kayaking down a river, think about how your body is moving and functioning to propel your kayak further. Allow yourself to be hyper aware of your muscles and movements, realizing a highly creative God is behind each action you take. If you go for a jog, let every footfall be part of a rhythm of gratitude. If you go on a hike, allow each step to be filled with wonder for how you can move through the beauty of the world with fresh air in your lungs. As you stretch and move, reflect on how God made each part of you, knitting you together with care, intention, and in His image.

Get creative with what will help keep you moving and active. Sometimes it's little things like a great playlist, a new pair of cute shoes, or a gorgeous view that can turn a ho-hum exercise experience into a mentally and physically refreshing

---

3. 2 Corinthians 4:16-18

activity. Shift your mind to things from above and celebrate the blessing of all that you are able to do! This transforms exercise from something that is monotonous to an act of worship. Taking good care of our physical selves is a way to demonstrate gratitude to God.

The Meanest Mean Girl

You can work earnestly to seek faith-informed beauty and then all of a sudden, a mean girl starts to unravel your sweet sense of confidence. It happens when you hear things like, "That shirt doesn't look good on you. I'm pretty sure you've put on a couple pounds." Or maybe you hear, "Your forehead is huge! I wouldn't pull your hair back in a ponytail, it just makes it more obvious!" There's also those deeper jabs that go beyond the physical into the core of who we are, "You really are too much for most people. Too intense and extra! That's why you don't have a lot of friends"

Those are all such unkind words, horribly mean! They undermine who you are and whose you are because they emphasize your imperfections and cut you down.

Who is this mean girl that has the audacity to say those ugly things? She's the internal mean girl. The one that lives in the space between your ears. The meanest mean girl is often found within our own thought life and self-talk. We are often the meanest mean girl in our life.

Everything I've shared are mean girl insults I've hurled at myself from time to time. They range from small nitpicks of my physical appearance to critiques of my personality and value. The list could go on and on. Like so many women I fight to control my thought life, taking it captive and seeing myself as God sees me. It's really frightening how easy it is to talk unkind to ourselves.

Do you realize that in John 10:10 we are given the heads up that the evil one has come to "steal and kill and destroy?" What better way to accomplish this destruction than within your thought life and self-concept? The evil one relishes any opportunity to purport the lie that you are not enough— not pretty enough, young enough, fit enough, skinny enough, trendy enough, cute enough, and the list goes on.

These lies about who you are kill your sense of peace and confidence. As your self-confidence is destroyed, making you feel anything but lovely, your shine begins to dim. You shrink back as you feel inadequate, which is the exact opposite of what this world needs. Think of the freedom you would find if you cast aside your mean inner dialogue and instead embraced loving and faith-based affirmations.

How do you stop the negative inner dialogue?

Step one is calling out your inner mean girl. You can't make her stop if you don't expose the nasty things she's up to. Often, I'll talk to my husband about it and mention I'm feeling insecure in my own skin or that I'm wrestling with some tough things. He is great about diffusing it with a joke, compliment, or reminder about how he loves me. If he isn't around in my moment of inner-meanness I dig in to fight on my own. It's as simple as saying to myself, "Well that was mean!" Calling the meanie out is important!

Step two, which might be the most eye opening of the steps, is imagining saying that same unkind thing to your mom, sister, best friend or daughter. If you shudder in horror at saying such ugly things out loud, to another person, it's clear the thought has got to go. It makes zero sense that you would say things to yourself that I would never say to another woman. Holding yourself accountable in this way is sobering.

Step three is being intentional about speaking kindly to yourself. It's a habit you need to develop. It's a muscle you need to flex and grow. Therefore, it takes commitment and work. Notice when you feel confident and lovely. Instead of letting that be a fleeting moment and passing thought, stay there and linger. Allow yourself to smile as you realize that you are in a sweet place of confidence. Celebrate the kindness you are showing to yourself as you allow your inner dialogue to be uplifting. As you emphasize this type of self-talk your inner mean girl is going to find there is less and less space for her between your ears.

> Notice when you feel confident and lovely. Instead of letting that be a fleeting moment and passing thought, stay there and linger.

This world needs you to shine bright! You cannot let your inner mean girl be used as a covert agent of evil—fight back and take every thought captive!

> Action Item: Take out your Bible and read through Psalm 139 fully. Read it slowly, allowing the power of each word to wash over you and take root in your mind and heart.

A Struggle to Be Lovely and Fierce

As you may have guessed, when it comes to being both lovely and fierce, I have a real tendency toward being fierce. I have an intensity about me as it relates to my belief in right and wrong. I thirst for justice and don't back down from fights. In fact, I wonder if my police training rewired my fight or flight instincts to be almost exclusively fight. At times, my ability to be both lovely and fierce becomes incredibly difficult and something I can only navigate through clinging to God and His guidance for me.

This struggle often shows up as I advocate for our son. He's a non-normative learner in the classroom, which creates many challenges. In order to ensure we are setting him up for success, I regularly have to step in to advocate for him because he's too young to fully self-advocate at this time.

His learning challenges have required a delicate balance of choosing a disposition of kindness and graciousness, while also being a warrior on his behalf. We are so fortunate that the educators in our area are fantastic beyond words and have a genuine love for our son. We are spoiled by teachers and leaders with huge hearts, lots of experience, and deep care for each child. Simultaneously, we have been entrusted to care for our son and it's our responsibility to fight for his needs as we seek to optimize his learning experience.

I know the education team is used to me at this point. They know I'm an active and engaged member of his learning. I even start my emails with "Hi Team"—because I really do see us as a collaborative group with the shared goal of helping our son be his best self. Most of the time, we have feelings of camaraderie and togetherness, but in very rare instances I've felt myself shift into a more primal role—a momma bear role.

Hard moments and challenging conversations happen as his educational team seeks to meet his needs while balancing very real constraints. Recently, we bumped into a situation that left me feeling seething and sad. My love for our son and heartbreak over a classroom situation pushed me into an emotional place I don't go often—but I did that day. It's only by the grace of God I had the wherewithal to not do or say anything until I calmed down. I called my husband, processed on the phone with him, took a deep breath, and got myself together.

I must confess, there are times when the lovely in me is overshadowed by the fierce. I'm not proud of this and I don't think it's where God wants me to be. As mommas, we really need to watch out for this. We can't forget that we are first a daughter of the King and second a mother to our children. We may feel our animalistic reactions are justified because as momma bears, that's just what we do. If you don't have children, you may relate to the feeling when you consider your love for your siblings, best friend, or spouse. As much as we want to justify our emotions and reactions, as women of faith we do things differently. Remember, we are pursuing justice, asked to love mercy, and instructed to walk humbly.[4]

When we feel the primal urge rise from within our belly it's a sign to slow down, step away, and breathe deeply. When those strong feelings strike, wait before sending the email. Pause

---

4. Micah 6:8

before picking up the phone. Take a deep breath before opening your mouth to speak. Approach emotionally intense situations with a tactical and biblical response; "be quick to hear, slow to speak, slow to anger."[5] Don't forget who you are and whose you are. God values people and relationships, so you and I must do the same.

> Approach emotionally intense situations with a tactical and biblical response; be swift to hear, slow to speak, and slow to anger. Don't forget who you are and whose you are.

I know that I can't let my quest to advocate for our son outshine that primary calling on my life. I must intentionally seek to be lovely and fierce in this area.

In the situation that was so upsetting, with boiling emotions, I prayed earnestly before heading to the school for a meeting. I was so mad I didn't feel like praying, but I did it anyway. I told God that I was heartbroken and anxious, and I saw no path for resolution. Before asking Him to fix the situation I realized I needed Him to fix me. I experienced a swift miracle in my heart because by the time I pulled up to the school, a sense of calm washed over me. I remember sensing, "Just listen. Just listen. Just listen."

I met with one of my favorite educators and listened to the most honest, beautiful, transparent, and authentic words I could have hoped for. There was humility on both sides of the table and our shared love for my son quickly bound us together in that conversation. There were no adversaries, only advocates. There was no condemnation, only a cooperative and shared path forward.

---

5. James 1:19

I look back with gratitude for how I managed to be lovely and fierce that day. God was so gracious to course correct when I went down a momma bear path of anger and anxiety. I'm thankful that faith helped me work through my feelings and find the peace to walk into the meeting as a grace-filled advocate for our son.

God has a way of calming even the most ferocious momma bear. He is so good like that. Leaning into our faith over feelings has a way of flipping situations on their head and making a way when there is no identifiable path forward. It reminds me of God's promise to find beauty for our ashes.[6] That's what He did for me that day. What had become ugly and bleak was brought back to a place of beauty.

Are there ashes inside of you that need to be redeemed? I'm talking about the places you know are not lovely, not at all. Be honest with yourself. God already knows those dark corners are there. But He wants you to invite Him in.

Seek to soften the corners and edges that are cutting and undermine the beauty of who you are at your core. Trust God to make you over and as He does, your inner beauty will only grow.

Action Item: Spend time reflecting on areas of your life that you are allowing to be controlled by emotion rather than God's truth. How can you turn those feelings over with faith?

---

6. Isaiah 61:3

Brave and Bold Steps Forward

It's worth fighting to find your sense of lovely and fierce because you are worth it! I hope that you will commit to explore the complexities of how you can be both of these wonderful qualities.

1. What is an issue or cause that stirs up fierce feelings within you? How can you love mercy, walk humbly, and seek justice in this area?
2. On a scale of 1–10 how ferocious is your inner-mean girl? Spend time in honest reflection about how you can begin the work of taking every thought captive.
3. What is an area that you are tempted to move beyond "lovely and fierce" to become unrighteously fierce? How can you pray through this area and submit your intense feelings to God?
4. When do you feel the most lovely? What are you doing? Who are you with? What are you wearing? Take a moment to reflect on this.
5. Think about a woman you know who embodies both lovely and fierce. Take time to write about what you admire and how you observe these qualities. *(Bonus points if you reach out to her and share your kind words and affirmations!)*

CHAPTER 8

CONFIDENT AND HUMBLE

Confident. That is one word that I often hear others use to describe me. I wonder if I'm perceived as confident because I've held roles that are high-stakes and high-risk? I started as a police officer, transitioned into entrepreneurship, and later became a spokesperson and on-camera regular. I get it, those are all roles that I can objectively describe as requiring confidence. So, am I a generally confident person? Maybe. However, there is so much more to confidence than the outward facing roles we embody.

The word confidence is often perceived as meaning someone who is loud and outspoken, showy and daring. I don't agree with that assessment of the word. Often that is fake confidence, compensation for the deeply internal insecurities a person is navigating. True confidence can show up in big and bold ways, but I especially appreciate confidence that is secure enough to stay quiet, in the background, or defer to others. My definition of confidence is simply to be at peace with yourself.

When you are at peace with yourself you have a sense of calm about who you are. You are neither riled up about all your mistakes and weakness nor are you ego-driven and conceited. You are comfortable with the reality that God has equipped you with gifts, talents and passions while also recognizing that you have shortcomings and flaws. The most beautiful type of confidence is the kind that holds hands with humility.

Being humble is our beautiful ability to embody modesty in action. This quality reflects a spirit of deference to others and even will prioritize others before self. It's a servant-hearted posture of living and approaches situations with perspective beyond the end of your own nose. It sees others, values others, and seeks to bless others. A humble spirit means that you recognize others are worth it and wonderful too.

> A humble spirit means that you recognize others are worth it and wonderful too.

Admittedly, talking about the need for confidence is tricky when writing a faith-shaped book. Throughout scripture we are reminded over and over again to embody a humble spirit.[1] However, there is not a direct scripture reference to our sense of self-confidence. Although some may interpret it as "confidence is not godly" that is not accurate.

While there may not be an 11th command that says, "Thou shalt be confident" there is scriptural justification for having a sense of self that is rooted in who God says we are, which produces confidence. We are asked to let our light shine

---

1. 1 Peter 5:6, James 4:10

before others so that when the look at us, they see a bright billboard that reflects the glory of the Lord.[2] If you lack confidence and spend your life trying to dim your shine, you will not reflect the glory of God to your full potential. So yes, you should feel certain that who God made you to be is very important.

In finding our faith embedded in our identity in Christ we can find peace with ourselves. That peace allows us to move through life confidently. When our confidence comes from our relationship with Jesus, we become even more comfortable enacting the commands to love others, serve others, and approach life with humility. God is so gracious in how He has made the humble and confident pairing so powerful.

When you feel certain of your value, without feeling the need to prove it, you are more willing to try new things, serve others, and share your ideas. That is an impact-yielding, world-changing, life-giving combination. I'm so excited about you growing in your Jesus-rooted self-confidence! I feel energized just imagining all that will take place in your heart and mind over the next several pages.

Acute Insecurities

Have you heard of the impostor syndrome? I felt this syndrome long before I knew it had a name. Impostor syndrome is when you show up in a room and feel like you just don't quite belong. You may feel as if everyone else in the room has a skill set, experience, or intelligence that is superior to

---

2. Matthew 5:16

yours and at any moment they will expose you as a phony. Impostor syndrome is marked by intense feelings of insecurity and inadequacy. In a sense, it's feeling like a fraud.

I have personally felt impostor syndrome more times than I can count. Often, the intense waves of self-doubt wash over me when starting a new job or tackling a major project. The best way I can describe the feeling is comparing it to when I was a child, and I would play dress up in my mom's closet. The shoes were too big, and I was grabbing onto the excessive fabric of the clothes, but still trying to pull it off like it made sense. I was barely holding it all together but simultaneously trying to look like it all fit. That is a visual of what impostor syndrome feels like on the inside.

When I left law enforcement and pursued a career in marketing and communications I struggled with impostor syndrome, *bad*. I was genuinely afraid that people would ask about my background while at networking events. If you had checked my LinkedIn profile you would have seen no mention of my criminal justice degree, police academy training, or employment as a patrol officer. I feared that my less-than-traditional background would somehow detract from my legitimacy and credibility. Underneath all the success people were perceiving from the outside, my inner mean girl was telling me I was a fraud. I felt like I was tricking everyone around me. Isn't that horrible? What about you? Are there areas that you think far too lowly of yourself, to the point of self-deprecating thoughts that you are an impostor?

Impostor syndrome is often talked about with career-based situations in mind. It can transcend our workplaces and also show up in our personal lives. I often get impostor syndrome in big groups of ladies who are just hanging out. If it's a women's work event, I'm fine. However, if it's a personal get-together I find myself fighting insecurities. Although I try my best to be confident in who I am and who God made me to be, the human in me can slip into feeling like a fraud.

I recall one instance in which I was invited into a pool-side get-together at my friend's house. I knew her and one or two other women in attendance. I didn't clarify the attire or what I should bring because to me it was simple: it was a pool party! I thought it was going to be an opportunity for us to break the summer heat, while we splashed around and visited. Based on all these assumptions, I showed up ultra-casual, with my hair up in a messy bun, wearing a cover up over my bathing suit. I had my purse and a towel rolled up and tucked in my arm—I was ready for a cannonball!

Can you imagine my shock when I walked through the door and everyone was dressed in beautiful maxi dresses, their hair was perfectly curled, and their make-up was on point. I could tell people had been contouring their faces and applying ample amounts of hair spray to get those lovely beachy waves just right. They were not pool-ready, but I was!

At that moment, it wasn't the summer heat that made me sweat, it was the rush of impostor syndrome that washed over me. I was hit with massive insecurities that I clearly did not belong in their world. Because if I did, I wouldn't have made a silly assumption that the pool-side party was actually a pool party. I would have picked the perfect outfit and made sure to fix my hair before showing up. In that panicked pause, as I entered her house, I had a running inner dialogue with myself about all the reasons I shouldn't have even come. Before I knew it, I talked myself into feeling totally out of place and like an impostor at that get together.

Fortunately, the hostess is one of my favorite friends and as soon as I confessed my misinterpretation of the gathering, she burst into laughter. Since she found it so funny, I was able to relax and start to see the hilarity too. She offered to get her suit on and jump in the pool with me. In the end, she helped me confidently own my mistake and still have a whole lot of fun. My mistake then became a conversation piece and something to giggle over, as I made new friends. Also, I heard more than once, "I wish I had brought my suit." It reminded me that when we are insecure there are often others who are looking at us, feeling equally insecure, for different reasons.

When you feel like an impostor, fight the urge to flee. When this narrative of insecurity creeps into your mind you must take it captive. Breathe deeply and look at your situation from a bird's eye view. Try your very best to be objective! In my instance I could remember that I was invited to the party for a reason: the hostess wanted me there. My assumption about swimming was a reflection of my fun-loving spirit. Lastly, being the only one in a swimsuit was an opportunity for a funny opening as I got to know new women, an opportunity to not take myself too seriously. Finally, if other people made a big deal or judged that I wore a swimsuit to a pool-side party then they aren't my kind of people. #CANNONBALL

Unfortunately, our emotions can be some of the biggest liars we know! If we become overindulgent with our feelings, we run the risk of being controlled by them. Fight back by identifying the insecurities and intentionally combat them with truth—God's truth—about who you are. One of my favorite verses of scripture, that I cite more than once, is a reminder to take every single thought captive.[3] Don't let your thoughts and feelings take control of you and dictate your beliefs.

Unfortunately, our emotions can be some of the biggest liars we know! If we become overindulgent with our feelings, we run the risk of being controlled by them.

Your worthiness is not something that is determined by your clothing, degree, or title. We are not worthy based on how clean your house is or how well behaved your children are when you go out to dinner. Your value is not rooted in your ability to contour your makeup or how cute your maxi dress is. Your worthiness is far more deep, profound, and permanent than any of those things.

The ultimate declaration of your worthiness was God sending His only son to Earth to die for us and rise again so that we can enjoy a relationship with God now and forever.[4] There is nothing "impostor" about that—your value has been sealed for now and forever. If you can allow that powerful truth to take root in your heart it will change everything. Starting with your feelings of inadequacy. You can be filled with the power and the spirit of the Lord and therein lies the most compelling type of confidence.

Action Item: Pause and consider a situation in which you feel inadequate and insecure. At the core, what is causing you to feel this way? It's time to fight back! Take a deep breath and objectively respond to the insecurities with truth.

---

3. 2 Corinthians 10:5
4. John 3:16

A Chronic Lack of Confidence

Feeling like an impostor isn't the only way that a lack of confidence shows up. Instead of experiencing a lack of confidence in intense bursts, based on situations or circumstances, there are women who chronically have low self-esteem. As a result of their low self-esteem they spend much of their life trying to shrink themselves.

No, I'm not talking about some sci-fi laser beam device designed to make them ant sized. I'm talking about the ways they carry themselves, occupy space, speak, and live. Instead of standing tall, they figuratively and literally go through life hunched over and curled into themselves. They try to disappear.

This shows up when a woman has a really great idea but never shares it at work because she second guesses herself and talks herself out of it. She lacks the confidence to speak up and step into vulnerability. As a result, the idea is never considered and she's left wondering what might have been if she only had had the courage to speak up. She shrinks herself in meetings by holding back and not speaking up. As a result, her coworkers don't realize all the potential she has, and she isn't considered for larger roles and increased responsibilities.

The shrinking attempts also show up in more innocuous ways. With the language nuances we use. When we "just" want to ask a question or say "sorry, I have another question." We add little modifiers to our conversations that minimize and diminish our role in a conversation. Stop saying sorry! Stop "just" asking questions and boldly share what's on your mind! You are worth it, wonderful, and very deserving of standing tall, occupying space, and asking questions.

When we seek to "just" blend in and aim to hide in the literal and figurative corners of the room we are failing to bring our best into the world. We take on a type of humility that goes too far—so far that it hurts. God invites us to use our gifts and talents to bless the world and join His kingdom work in this world.[5] Shrinking and playing it small doesn't align with that directive. Remember, you are asked to be a billboard that reflects His glory to a world that desperately needs His hope. Let your light shine brilliantly before others![6]

If you are feeling like you have mastered the art of shrinking, I want you to know you are not alone. I have met a lot of women—too many women—who chronically struggle with confidence. There are still situations where I too have to fight for a healthy sense of confidence and resist the urge to shrink. There's no need for self-condemnation, but you can resolve to seek biblical confidence from this day forward.

As you seek to grow in confidence it's important to wash away your insecurities in a combination of scripture, prayer, and two practical steps forward.

First things first, start with scripture and prayer. In quiet moments, confess to God how you are feeling. Let Him know the areas of insecurities and the doubts you have about yourself. Spend time reading about who you are and the value you hold. Commit to believe it and claim it. I suggest you start with Psalm 139, a personal favorite of mine! Prioritize this pursuit before you proceed with any other next steps.

Often our eyes get fixated on what is in front of us in the moment and how defining it may feel. We walk into the

---

5. Romans 12:6-8
6. Matthew 5:16

room—literally or figuratively—and focus on all that we are not or the many ways we fall short. We look in the mirror and sigh with disappointment as we identify another gray hair or an additional wrinkle.

If you spend time critiquing yourself and wallowing in feelings of inadequacy what are you communicating to our Father about the work of His hand? Remember, the God of the Universe made you intentionally and personally. Your self-esteem matters for practical reasons and also for faith-shaped reasons.

Next, you need to pair this beautiful faith-reality with practical steps forward. Start by pausing and owning all that you have done and the journey you have already experienced. Sometimes we get so busy living that we forget all the life that has happened along the way. What have you overcome? What have you accomplished?

> Sometimes we get so busy living that we forget all the life that has happened along the way.

Take time to remember a really great idea you had that resulted in a major impact. Maybe it's simple and small, like a home improvement project. Or perhaps you bake award winning Blueberry Muffins—and if you do, I would like some! Maybe it's large and noteworthy, like a major work project or strategic initiative. Have you served your community or volunteered for an important cause? The experiences and examples are there, I'm sure of it.

While you reflect on all that you have accomplished and the skillsets you possess, I want you to intentionally link that back to how it's evidence of who God made you to be. Don't silo the two. You would not be an excellent project manager if He hadn't made you a logical and detail-oriented person. You wouldn't be an amazing coach if He hadn't given you a love for others and desire to mentor. You wouldn't have a propensity for hospitality and baking muffins if He hadn't blessed you in that area. When we connect our strengths to scripture we reframe confidence into a faith-shaped quality.

> Action Item: Write a list of the top 5 accomplishments you have achieved over your life. Next to the accomplishment, identify the God-given quality or skill set that has allowed you to achieve that. (Example: Publishing a book: God embedded a love for words within me.)

We can't forget that step 1, confidence in who God made us to be, is the reason that there is a step 2 to reflect on. Practical steps toward increased confidence are made possible by the faith-conviction that God is the reason you are worth it and wonderful. Pairing God's truth with reflection on your abilities and accomplishments is a recipe for biblical confidence.

A Quick Note on Compliments

Now that you have marching orders for embracing a faith-shaped confidence I want to urge you to apply it in a specific way, the way in which you receive compliments. Next time you are in a group of women and someone compliments the other, I want you to be curious about how the compliment is received. Is she able to simply allow it to wash over her with gratitude or does she try to make the compliment smaller by mitigating its power?

What about you? When someone gives you a compliment do you find yourself squirming and seeking ways to minimize the impact of what they just said? Here's a great example! Let's say you apply for a new job and are selected for the position. When your best friend reaches out to congratulate you your response is, "Yeah I'm excited, but the candidate pool was really small." Or maybe someone compliments your new haircut and instead of simply saying, "That's so nice of you to say!" You let them know, "I love the cut, but, oh my gosh, my hair is so frizzy today!"

Why is it so hard to simply receive a compliment with gratitude? Why do we feel squirmy when someone chooses to bless us with their words? This is another way that we try to shrink instead of standing tall.

To help fight the tendency toward diminishing compliments I have little phrases I use to graciously receive their words. I'll share my compliment-receiving toolkit with you, in hopes it helps you enjoy the sweet words without feeling the need to take away from the significance of what the other person is saying.

"Thank you for those kind words." I love this line! It affirms the other person while doing nothing to take away from their compliment. This line is pretty universal, keep it in your back pocket for the next time a compliment washes over you.

"That is such thoughtful feedback." This line works great when someone gushes about my work product or something performance based. It could be anything from "Wow, I love the blog article you wrote" to "You are such an engaged and hands-on mom." It affirms how kind they were to speak up and share.

"Your encouragement means so much!" Affirming that someone's words were life-giving will encourage them to continue with kindness and encouragement. Don't we want more people who speak goodness and kindness? Yes! So, when they do, let them know it matters.

Those are three of my favorite compliment-receiving phrases. I hope you'll use these phrases to help you get more and more comfortable with sweet words and kind feedback coming your way. Remember that you may have to use these phrases and force yourself to receive the compliment long before you feel totally comfortable doing it. It's important that you receive compliments well because we are supposed to encourage each other daily.[7] We are designed for community and to support each other through the twists and turns of life. When the kindness and support is focused on you, receive it well!

> **Action Item:** Find a friend and practice giving and receiving compliments. Cheesy? Maybe. Will it help you grow in confidence—yes!

Tombstone Confidence

Lacking confidence represents one extreme of the humble-and-confidence dynamic. The other extreme is a dangerously high level of confidence. While I think most women would say they wrestle with a lack of confidence, in specific situations I think ego-driven decision making can signal an abundance of confidence that lacks humility.

When I was in police academy an instructor warned me about Tombstone Courage. This catchy term describes a

---

7. Hebrews 3:13

reckless and potentially deadly characteristic. It describes an officer who charges in first and asks questions later. They don't pause to first gather information before taking action, which is perilous. It's actually not confidence at all but a desire to "prove" oneself. In their faux-courage and faux-confidence they make decisions with potentially harmful or deadly consequences.

For example, an officer may show up on scene and even though backup is only a minute out, they unnecessarily enter into the scene on their own. Yes, there are circumstances where you would rush in without backup, but that is usually unwarranted and unsafe. Failing to wait for backup exposes and officer to increased danger and the opportunity to be seriously hurt. With nobody to watch their back or offer a second set of eyes there is an enhanced probability for detrimental outcomes. If the situation allows time to wait, gather more support, and move in a measured way, it makes so much more sense to do so.

I believe that in the broader landscape of life we can have Tombstone Confidence. This is a type of extreme confidence that lacks humility. In fact, it transcends confidence and becomes pride-driven decision making and living. It's a "charge ahead now" mentality. It can rear its ugly head in our workplaces, relationships, and friendships. Tombstone Confidence is stubborn, unyielding and can be fatal to friendships and relationships.

Tombstone Confidence shows up when a supervisor refuses to receive hard feedback about how she can better support employees. She charges ahead arrogantly and acts like it's the employee's problem and refuses to take any amount of ownership. She prioritizes nurturing her pride over nurturing her team. As a result, her leadership footing at work begins to erode.

It also shows up as a parent who refuses to apologize to their children for mistakes made. Tombstone Confidence clings to a false narrative that parents are always right and children are just too young and naive to understand. Prideful parenting will chip away at the precious relationship she could have with her children, all because she's stubborn and unyielding.

Tombstone Confidence is also evident in the friend who decides to cut another friend off instead of working through conflict. Rather than entering into a tough conversation she chooses to pass judgment and create distance. Being right and protecting her ego is a hill she's willing to let the friendship die on. She will stubbornly stand firm and call it principle-based when really it's pride-based.

Tombstone Confidence charges ahead without pausing to ask questions, have the hard conversation or consider other information. In the immediacy, it may seem easier, but it lacks humility and is destructive over the long term. This type of prideful confidence lacks the willingness to accept you can do better, be better, or improve. It takes the posture of rightness to the point of lacking righteousness.

Like so much of life, it comes down to our true identity found in Christ. When we realize that our worth is bigger than our mistakes, we are able to stop living in an ego-driven way. Being certain that our worth is rooted in who God says we are sets us free from the need to pursue reckless confidence.

It takes true confidence to utter the words, "I was wrong" without feeling self-inflicted shame and condemnation. With a faith-shaped sense of confidence that is washed in humility we can live with assurance that our value remains intact all the same. God does not give us leeway when it comes to conflict and maintaining healthy relationships. Indulging our pride leaves a wake of destruction, guard your heart against this![8]

Sober Self-Assessment

Confidence rooted solely in ourselves is a problem. Humility that undermines our God-given value is also a problem. A stark awareness of who God made us to be and the depths of His majesty and love is how we can work toward a solution. It's how we can be both confident and humble.

When thinking about how to illustrate this idea of being confident and humble I can call to mind an ironic recurring dream of mine. In my dream, I learn that I have been selected to appear on American Idol. I go through the process of hair and make-up, selecting my wardrobe, and then am whisked away to the dress rehearsal. I show up to rehearsal and am stunned to realize that I cannot sing. Not in the slightest.

The rest of my dream is trying to figure out what song I could sing that would help me endure the experience with some measure of dignity remaining on the other side of the performance. I consider all the options and if there's a song that will let me trick everyone into thinking I can actually sing.

I always wake up from the dream so perplexed because even in slumber-state I'm strikingly aware that I have not been gifted with a melodious singing voice. It's a good thing I know my strengths and skill set are limited in this

8. Proverbs 16:18

area because it means I will never travel to a major city to stand in line for American Idol. I'll also never volunteer to serve in the worship band at church. You will also never find me up on stage, singing Karaoke. I'm very sure that this is an area of weakness. Not only am I sure of it, I own it!

Just as it helps to be confident about the strengths and talents I possess, it's also helpful to be certain of my areas of weakness. It brings about clarity about how God has equipped me to serve and shine and helps me know what opportunities I should pursue—and which ones (like singing competitions) are not going to result in a golden ticket. Owning our weaknesses does not diminish our shine or God-given value. Rather, it clarifies our God-given strengths and helps us know how we should amplify those areas.

> Owning our weaknesses does not diminish our shine or God-given value. Rather, it clarifies our God-given strengths and helps us know how we should amplify those areas.

I've never taken voice lessons and don't plan to because I recognize that this is not a way I'm going to impact the world for good. Since I know my singing is a lost cause I don't waste time thinking about it or trying to get better in this area. Instead, I focus my time and attention on areas that I'm certain God has gifted me. For example, I spend time reading leadership books and books on social justice because I have a heart for fighting for the vulnerable and am drawn to leadership roles. I seek to refine and sharpen a skillset and passion that I'm sure is God-given.

This awareness of our strengths and weaknesses is addressed within Romans 12:3 (NIV) as "sober judgment" of ourselves.

This is a biblical way of describing the importance of not thinking too highly or too lowly of yourself.

Let me apply this concept to my not-made-for-Idol example. If I let my inability to sing make me feel like I was all around worthless and lacking in talent I would be taking on a self-assessment that is too lowly. Alternatively, if I refused to acknowledge that my singing voice is something only my mother could love, I'm lacking in humility. Focusing on our weaknesses and beating ourselves up over them is not a way to live with faith-shaped confidence. Confidence in my God-given strengths must be met with a humble acceptance that I'm flawed and lacking in some areas.

Aim to be sober minded about who you are and your worth, sure of your strengths and content with your weaknesses.

Action Item: Read Romans 12:3–13. Spend time reflecting about your self-assessment and if it could be described as "sober." Consider if the work ahead requires an increased measure of confidence or fostering a more humble spirit.

Humble Yourself with Service

Are you good at throwing pity parties? I have my moments. There are times where I start feeling sorry for myself and instead of allowing it to be fleeting, I indulge the feelings. In a very bizarre irony, this is a way of elevating myself and failing to prioritize the needs of others. Simply put, I can't see beyond the end of my own nose. I turn inward and forget to focus my eyes on God's perspective and also fail to be attentive to the needs of those around me.

Anytime we find ourselves with such limiting tunnel vision we are entering dangerous territory. The Bible is full of passages in which we are told to love others through service, to pray for others, lift them up, and to live with an open hand. This is our call to live humble lives that, "count others more significant" than ourselves.[9] Overindulging our emotions is counterproductive to this call.

In allowing our needs and challenges to become all consuming, we live self-centered lives. This is exactly why my anecdote to a pity party is intentionally serving someone else.

This is the kingdom perspective and upside-down logic that is found throughout the Bible. Often, the very thing that sounds illogical is what results in profound blessing. The first will be last and the last will be first; lift the needs of others and in the process, you will be lifted.[10]

When you find yourself hurting deeply or in a raging pity party, seek enough self-awareness to call yourself out and identify a path forward. Who can you love well at that moment? It could be as simple as sending a text of encouragement to a friend. Or you could bake blueberry muffins and drop them off at a neighbor's house (or my house!). As you seek to humble yourself in service to others the Lord will bless you. He will remind you just how special it is for you to recognize that others are worth it and wonderful too. The boomerang blessings will follow. You simply cannot love others well without experiencing blessings in return.

9. Philippians 2:3-4
10. Matthew 20:16

> You simply cannot love others well without experiencing blessings in return.

The world tells you that you should feel what you need to feel and affirms that your emotions are okay. To an extent, that is true. There is nothing wrong with having challenging days, going through the process of grief, or struggling with negative emotions. By no means am I advocating for "stuffing" feelings down and ignoring the painful emotions that swirl. I'm all for processing! However, there comes a time when processing needs to be taken captive in order to continue walking in faith. Your emotions can't control and consume you to the point that you fail to live in alignment with God's commands.

As you seek to be a bright light in a broken world you have to remember there are big stakes for how you process and proceed through life. People are watching. They are curious about who God is to you. They will notice your confidence—or lack thereof and they will also notice how you humbly serve others—or don't.

You are important—so are they.
Your needs matter—so do theirs.
You deserve special gestures of love—so do they.

Treat others the way you deserve and want to be treated and watch what God does next. Live beyond yourself and experience the blessings that follow. Embrace humility.

Always Remember

The paradox of being confident and humility is a fantastic one to explore. There are layers and layers to the challenges and opportunities we find within this pair. As we get to the end of this chapter, I want to encourage you to *always remember*.

"Remember what?" you may ask.

I want to you to remember God's faithfulness to you over the duration of your life. Life is a lot less scary and insecurities are a lot less powerful when this perspective shapes all your perceptions. Remember how God has walked with you each and every step of the way.

When you become so confident in His magnificence and majesty you will realize that you have less to be insecure about. Fuse these truths with the realization that He knows this world needs you, too. A big mighty God made little ole you—and He is so glad He did.

> When you become so confident in His magnificence and majesty you will realize that you have less to be insecure about.

The Old Testament has oodles of references to remembering. It seems that this is one of the things God wanted His people, the Israelites, to do most often. Maybe it was because they seemed to have amnesia about all the ways that He was meeting their every need and equipping them across their life journey. God would provide and they would forget. In their forgetfulness they would default to fear, anxiety and insecurities. They lacked confidence.

Like them, I'm prone to amnesia too. Left to my own human-ways, I default to forgetting all that God has done and the ways He shows up in the details. Remembering is a choice and something I seek to get better at. I hope you'll join me in a quest to remember.

A practical way I do this is by jotting down realizations, answered prayers, challenges, and joys in my journal. I don't have a legalistic approach to journaling; I write as I feel inspired and led. Even in my sporadic documentation I have a beautiful running history of how God has shown up with provision time and time again. It's so special to look back and see how He was making a way, when no way seemed possible.

I have other practical ways I apply scriptural truth about God's provision as a means of building confidence. A specific and tangible thing I do is read Exodus 20:2 and then make it personal for my own life. This verse is a huge moment in scripture, right before God provided Moses with the ten commandments. Right before He did, God reminded them, "I am the Lord your God, who brought you out of the land of Egypt, out of the house of slavery." He preempts a hugely significant portion of the Old Testament with a reminder to remember.

On my days of doubts, when impostor syndrome makes me feel in over my head, or when I'm not sure I fit in with others, I personalize this scripture to bring me back to a God-rooted reality.

I am the Lord your God who delivered you from melanoma.
I am the Lord you God who blessed you with a pregnancy when man said it was not possible.
I am the Lord your God who blessed you with a business.
I am the Lord your God who invited you into ministry with New Hope Girls.

I am the Lord your God who has given you your gifts, talents, and quirks.

I am the Lord your God who has loved you your entire life. Never giving up on you.

When I remember who the Lord *my* God is, I have every reason to stand fully confident and fully humble before Him.

Please take time to read Exodus 20:2 and personalize it for your journey. Don't forget the many ways that the Lord your God has shown up for you. Make it intimate as you reflect on the ways He has revealed Himself to you, through the blessings and the struggles. In this exercise, it's my sincere prayer that a new level of confidence will take root in your heart. The confidence that comes only from our good and beautiful God.

Action Item: Take time to remember. Fill in the blank, "I am the Lord your God who _____."

Brave and Bold Steps Forward

I'm excited for you to walk through the coming days with a greater sense of confidence and also a humble spirit! I hope these prompts help you take your first steps in that direction.

1. Write a list of the 10 things you love most about yourself. Use this list as a way to celebrate who God made you to be.
2. When have you experienced the most intense feelings of impostor syndrome?
3. Call to mind a time you selflessly served someone else. What did you learn or gain from that experience?

4. Take a pulse check on your pride. Are there areas of your life you need to embrace a more humble disposition?

5. How can you grow a deeper sense of confidence because of God's proven faithfulness in your life?

CHAPTER 9

INDEPENDENT AND SUPPORTED

As a former cop and entrepreneur, I'm all-too familiar with the rush that comes from knowing I'm highly independent. However, independence as a consistent state of being is not long-term sustainable or healthy. As human beings, we have a God-given need for relationships and community. A truly healthy person is both independent and interdependent, able to take care of herself while also relying on others for support when necessary.

As I've taken more and more trips around the sun, I have realized how critical it is for me to allow others to serve and support me. In order to live the most meaningful and fulfilling life I have to rely on others. For a stubborn, strong-willed and impatient person, like me, this is a challenging lesson to learn and fully receive.

An important aspect of living bravely and

> An important aspect of living bravely and boldly is choosing to be both independent and supported by others.

boldly is choosing to be both independent and supported by others.

A Major Moment of Need

After struggling to get pregnant I was enamored by the experience of growing a little person inside my body. I immersed myself in the world of all things pregnancy, from health and nutrition to nursery planning and maternity fashion. I could not believe something so miraculous was happening to me and within me.

One day while I was experiencing pregnancy back pain, my husband graciously gave me a back rub. While he was doing so, he commented on a mole on my lower back that looked "weird." It was in the middle of my lower back and regardless of the acrobatics I tried to perform, I could barely even see that it existed. I was around 25 weeks pregnant, so my protruding stomach made it all the more cumbersome to bend and twist. My husband made it clear that he felt *strongly* that I ask the OBGYN to take a look at that weird spot on my back during my next baby check-up.

I'm pretty averse to going to the doctor and pregnancy only amplified this aversion. I despised all the appointments, exams, and needle sticks that accompanied pregnancy. I was highly annoyed by my husband's request regarding the mole on my back. I didn't want even one more thing to talk about at my next appointment.

Eventually my doctor saw the spot and instantly said, "you need to see a dermatologist." I thought she was over-reacting and was patronizing me because I was pregnant. In my fantasyland, I had believed the dermatologist would soon take my side and rescue me from yet another medical intervention.

All I wanted was a happy and simple pregnancy—I wanted it to be perfect and with no additional stressors. Maybe you have also been in a blissful situation in which you sensed things were finally going to work out—and then they didn't.

I can recall feeling disoriented but also deeply disappointed when my dermatologist said the spot needed to be removed immediately. At that point in my life I'd never had surgery, stitches or a broken bone. I was a medical newbie and found the biopsy procedure to be overwhelming. After I got over my initial overwhelm, I was just plain mad. Do you also get mad when life doesn't unfold as you feel it should?

My nightmare phone call came a couple weeks after the biopsy. I was chatting with a coworker when my dermatologist's number come across my phone. As I attempted to listen to Dr. Johnston, I learned I had melanoma and it had advanced down into my body, so it was no longer "in situ" or only within the top layer of my skin. However, my pathology was otherwise really great. He reviewed the various features of my melanoma and emphasized that with an aggressive surgery he had every reason to believe I'd be okay.

I was shattered by the news: breathless, overwhelmed, flooded with thoughts, questions, and fears.

Through my tears and questions Dr. Johnston was so kind. I remember saying, "What about my baby? Will I be able to see her go to kindergarten someday?" It was such a strangely specific question, but it was also reflective of my deep desire to watch her grow, develop, and learn. I wanted to see her get on the bus—full of excitement and potential. I craved the "everyday normal" of raising our child, alongside my husband. I was so afraid for her, on top of being afraid for me.

CHAPTER 9

I was furious that life wasn't unfolding as it was supposed to. I expect you might also know that feeling. Isn't it miserable when you wait so long for a moment and then all of a sudden darkness is trying to encroach on your joy? That is what made me so mad—pregnancy was supposed to be a dream come true experience. It was not supposed to be another nightmare.

The bottom dropping out can leave us feeling abandoned and unseen by God. This is the moment that support must come alongside us and wrap us up in love that affirms truth.

Have you experienced unexpected news that leaves you grasping to hold on? This type of jarring news can leave you feeling untethered to planet Earth and lost in a vast expanse. All of a sudden, your world is unfamiliar, and every hope and dream seems laughable in the face of the information you are facing. That is where I found myself.

Life-altering medical news is always hard to receive, but I quickly learned that it's even harder to share. I called my parents and they instantly dropped what they were doing to come to get me and drive me home. I really struggled to call my husband. He was preparing to work a midnight shift that night and I kept saying, "I can't wake him, he needs to rest." While it sounded like a valid reason not to call him, it wasn't my true motivator. The reality was that the only thing worse than receiving the diagnosis was having to tell my husband.

A coworker, Wendi, came and waited with me until my parents made it to my work to drive me home. Wendi was also pregnant at the time, and we became fast friends and navigated our pregnancies together. To this day I remember her presence. I have no recollection of the specific words she said, if any, or what she did other than show up and stay with me. That was the most powerful thing she could have

164

done. She sat quietly and was comfortable in my presence, even though I was a total wreck. That was what I desperately needed in that moment, a person to hold space for me.

Driving home with my mom and dad I remember feeling their strength surrounding me. I was finally able to call my husband and tell him what I had learned. I heard his sweet assurance that it would all be okay and we would take it one step at a time.

My husband went to work long enough to sit down with his supervisor and share the news and discuss what he would need in the days to come. I remember when he left for that brief trek into the office, I hugged his neck and cried saying I didn't want to be alone. While he was at work, I went and got dinner with my parents. I still remember where we went, what I ate, and that the cheesy potato soup had lost its taste. Sitting with my diagnosis initially turned me inward and numbed my senses.

After dinner, we went to Target, and I bought a "bravery scarf." It was a bold red-orange color and became the accessory I wore to all of my melanoma appointments to come—a silent expression of my will to stand strong in the face of melanoma.

My work family was gracious and followed my lead on what I needed, which for me was a sense of normalcy. I returned to the office after my meeting with the surgeon because I didn't want to sit alone in my struggle.

Surgery happened one-week after my diagnosis. I was hospitalized in advance due to high blood pressure. I remember laying in the hospital bed, waiting for surgery to happen, and two of the staff members from our church came to visit me and pray with us. I remember my mom as a strong and steady presence throughout the hospitalization and waiting. I also remember my mother-in-law visiting and bringing me a children's book, "The Kissing Hand" that I could (and would) later give to our daughter. She climbed right into the hospital bed with me and read the book out loud. I felt surrounded and supported by those who love me.

As I was wheeled back for surgery my husband gave me a small slip of paper with a note and Bible verse written, reminding me he was always with me, even in the operating room. I still have that token of his love and support, to this day, sandwiched between the pages of my Bible.

Fear not, for I am with you;
   be not dismayed, for I am your God;
I will strengthen you, I will help you,
   I will uphold you with my righteous right hand.
Isaiah 41:10

I love that my husband pointed me to God and gave me truth to hold onto—literally—when so much felt overwhelming. This is the best first step we can take when we get the phone call we were praying against. Grab onto truth and don't let go!

A week after I had a biopsy, I was in the surgery bay. In the weeks to come I learned that the surgery was a success! Further testing indicated that we had every reason to believe the melanoma was fully removed and I should have a healthy prognosis moving forward.

I still have copies of the emails that were exchanged between me and my friends, both near and far, during that trying time. From time to time I read those emails again, as a beautiful reminder of how God is so gracious. One email was written to my mom, early in the morning, as I struggled to sleep in between the diagnosis and surgery. I poured my heart out.

> *Hey Mom! I didn't sleep hardly at all last night...I just can't get my head to stop and calm down. I'm doing okay enough but am having a hard time again. I just keep reminding myself "I can trust God no matter what" I'm just scared of what today will bring and so scared for my baby and I'm getting ready to get in the shower. I'm just listening to a few praise songs and trying to get my head on straight. I'm just so scared is all. Sometimes life is just too painfully real.*

When life is too painful and overwhelming, and battles are raging, we have to cling to our God-given community and allow others to lift us up. It reminds me of one of my favorite Old Testament accounts of Moses, Aaron and Hur. In Exodus 17 the Israelites are engaged in a raging battle, but God is with them. God commands Moses to raise his arms, and in doing so, the Israelites will be victorious. However, a problem arises when Moses gets tired and he can no longer hold up his arms. In God's graciousness, He makes a way. Aaron and Hur find a rock for Moses to sit on and then each of them holds up one of his arms, allowing the Israelites to achieve victory within the battle.

Action Item: Go read Exodus 17:8–16 and reflect on when you have been "Aaron and Hur" to a friend or family member in your life. Similarly, consider who has been your "Aaron and Hur" during one of your life battles.

Looking back on the entire cancer experience, I never felt alone. I was flanked by my own Aarons and Hurs each and every step. From those early moments when Wendi sat with me, to my parents picking me up and driving me home. My husband consistently "held up my hands" as I navigated this battle. God provided me with the sweet and strong community I needed to engage the health battle of melanoma and emerge victorious. Not only was I victorious physically, but I also navigated the experience with an emotional strength that defies logic. I was pressed but not crushed by the diagnosis.[1]

Truthfully, it wasn't always easy to receive their help. At that point in my life, I was a fiercely independent woman used to "saving the day" for others as a police officer. I proudly wore my independent persona and prided myself in my self-perceived strength. I did this to a fault. Then came melanoma and I was brought to my knees.

Experiencing melanoma while pregnant reminded me I'm human, vulnerable and with valid needs that can only be met by others. The harsh realities of cancer educated me on the reality of true strength. True strength is found in our ability to both give and receive support.

> True strength is found in our ability to both give and receive support.

My experience with cancer was a stand-out moment of the need for reliance on others. It was a life altering experience and left me feeling far more blessed than frustrated. Although I would never willingly sign up for a diagnosis like that, I'm truly grateful for the blessings it ushered into my life. Melanoma took nothing from me and with a strong support

---

1. 2 Corinthians 4:8-10

system, I gained so much through the fight. That is just proof of God's glory and His ability to take the hardest parts and use them for good.[2] He does indeed have plans for us!

Consider your own pain and hardships and a moment that may have brought you to your knees. When you look back on the challenging time, who was there? Who did God surround you with? Who blessed you with service and love? If you can see their face right now, I hope you will make a point to let them know of their impact. Vocalize how God used them to support and love you.

The Gift of Support

Since that diagnosis I've had to continue to grow my ability and willingness to ask for, accept, and receive help. However, I also still love the feeling of being independent. This is one example of two competing characteristics I still struggle to fully embrace.

I cycle through seasons where I start to believe the lie that independence should be prized above reliance and that asking for help makes me needy or weak. The truth is, asking for help makes me human, part of a community and affirms how cherished I am by others.

Think back on the last time you did something selfless for another person. Did you make a casserole for a new mom? Did you pause your workday to really listen to a coworker experiencing a struggle? Maybe you volunteered within the community, to intentionally serve others. Pause, close your eyes, and reflect on how it felt.

---

2. Romans 8:28

Did you feel the warmth that comes from loving others well? I know that any time I serve others, and allow them to rely on me, I'm left feeling a touch guilty over how much I gained from the service experience. You can't love others well without reaping the benefits yourself. The return on your investment in others is one that always pays dividends.

Knowing how good it feels to serve, why would you rob others of that gift? Why would you not lean into them, allowing them an opportunity to affirm your value and lift you up? It's when we are vulnerable that we connect most deeply with others.

We are expected to open our hands wide in support of each other.[3] We are to serve each other as the hands and feet of Jesus. Although living a life of service cannot be overlooked as believers, we also have examples of how we should allow ourselves to be served and loved by our community.

One of the most beautiful interactions between Jesus and His disciples occurred as He served them, washing their feet.[4] Not only did this demonstrate the humble character of Jesus, and give us an example of how to love others, but it also showed us that there are times we need to allow ourselves to be served.

There were times during my cancer ordeal that people offered to bring me meals and my first inclination was to refuse the help. I reasoned that we could grab takeout or make an oven baked pizza. After more thought, I realized that it wasn't really about the food. Accepting the food was about receiving the gift of community, welcoming others to

---

3. Deuteronomy 15:11
4. John 13:1-17

pour into our lives and lift us up. By saying "yes" we gave them the gift of feeling fulfilled because living beyond ourselves provides deep soul-satisfaction. When we say yes to help from others, we allow ourselves to love and be loved. "I need help" are three of the bravest words we can ever say.

If you find yourself hesitating to receive help, I hope you will remember that God is the sender of all our help. Let Psalm

> When we say yes to help from others, we allow ourselves to love and be loved.

121:1 swirl through your mind: "I lift up my eyes to the hills. From where does my help come? My help comes from the Lord, who made heaven and earth." Maybe it will help you receive help when you recognize the blessing of their support as a direct gift from above. I urge you to allow yourself to be loved in this profound way. And while you do so, offer up a prayer of gratitude as you recognize the support as a good and perfect blessing from above.

Your Balcony People

We need support in so many ways, not just physical and practical needs. As you wrestle with big dreams and challenges within your life you need a core group of people who will journey with you. Your hopes and dreams also need to be surrounded and supported by your community.

There will be times when your belief wavers and you question yourself or you question absolutely everything. I've been there. Across various life stages and career stops I have wrestled with doubts and even fear of the future. I've had multiple times in which I felt in over my head.

CHAPTER 9

Sometimes I can fight the doubts, questions and insecurities on my own. But when I'm not able to, I have to call in reinforcements. I need backup to fact-check the stories and narratives that are silently bouncing around my brain. I contact someone from my balcony and ask them to speak truth into my life. What do I mean by my balcony?

Imagine a beautiful and ornate stage. Usually, there is a balcony on either side of the stage that offers a unique and up-close vantage point for all that transpires on the stage. The view from the balcony provides perspective and clarity.

Your balcony people are your elite group of supporters.

I have balcony people in my life who have a unique and up-close vantage point as I continue forward on each stage of life. They are the first to rise to their feet for a standing ovation and they are the first to shed tears with me when things are tough. They are also the individuals willing to speak the hard truth in my life, when needed. These are the reinforcements I call in when my belief is wavering, my days feel hard, and my dreams feel out of reach.

Continuing the performance analogy, consider how some people watch a play and can't stop raving about the musical score. Whereas others immediately launch into a critique over the plausibility of the plot line. And then there are those who comment on the staging, costumes and makeup. Each person has an area of focus and observations that are meaningful to the performance. This multifaceted perspective is what you want in your balcony!

There should be diverse perspectives in your balcony so that you have a varied community of support for the many ups and downs, challenges and opportunities of life. The best balconies have people with different areas of expertise and perspectives. No one person can be your entire balcony!

My balcony has a variety of people with different perspectives. Front and center is my husband, who is wise, practical, discerning and highly disciplined. If I need help with logistics, he's my man! If I need help with a creative direction, he's not the guy for the job. For that, I usually turn to my sister-in-law, Kate.

Speaking of Kate ...

There was one day I was feeling really discouraged about the slow pace at which my dreams were progressing. I felt as if I was out of touch with reality in thinking I could make an impact or achieve something that seemed like a stretch goal. The worst of impostor syndrome was setting in. My sister-in-law Kate had no idea what I was wrestling with and that an ugly lie of inadequacy started to take root in my mind. Out of the blue, she sent an email, truly a love letter, to lift me up and share her belief in me.

I love you. I love that you're raising a daughter who wonders and dreams just as big as her mom. More importantly, I love that you love yourself first—for this is the hardest and greatest thing a woman can do. Thank you for always showing up. Use your power of presence to give others permission and inspiration to do the same!

I heard a question today that stopped me and gave me real pause. I wanted to share it with you. "The question is not 'What do I want from life?'; it's 'what does life ask of me?'"

Don't just have a career—find a calling. Why are you here and where can Caitlyn make the most of her God-given leadership, strength, prose, and power?

As I read through this sweet love letter over and over, I shed tears that were healing and clarifying.

My balcony person, my sister-in-law, reminded me who I am and WHOSE I am. I'm a daughter of the King with beautiful blessings and beautiful dreams. It was the perspective reset I needed, and she provided it at just the right time. I fully believe that her letter was God directly using her to provide a sweet, sweet gift. Remember, every good and perfect gift we experience is from God.[5]

Take a moment and consider, who are your balcony people? They are for you, and they are your champions. They are the fact-checkers who will provide clarity and truth when your inner narrative gets off track. They are the ones that are in it with you, for the long haul. They are for you and want your best. What's your balcony looking like these days?

Spotlight Moment

We don't always find ourselves on a literal stage, with a literal balcony of people watching a performance unfold. We often live this reality in a more analogous sense. However, at one point I did find myself standing on a big stage with a spotlight focused in my direction. All thanks to an audacious dream and some big ideas!

At some point I had a bold dream that I wanted to give a TEDx talk. It even felt a "little much" to me, when the idea popped into my brain. I think my oldest brother Josh was largely to thank for the dream. He loves to send me TED talks and other thought-provoking videos and ideas. One day

5. James 1:17

I remember thinking, "Why not me!?" The dream developed largely because I knew it would push me way past my comfort zone and I loved the rush that I got when thinking about attempting something seemingly impossible.

I wanted to chase something wild. I also wanted a bigger stage for impact. I craved the opportunity to stand on a stage, on my own two feet, and move an audience. To be clear though, it wasn't just about "proving it" to myself. I was driven by the belief that I had a message worth sharing and this was a special opportunity to encourage others.

Through a series of serendipitous events (which by serendipitous I mean "God made it happen in a way only He can!") I ended up interacting with a student who was part of the TEDx team at Virginia Commonwealth University. I had never considered applying to that nearby university to give a talk, but through that connection I realized that maybe, *just maybe*, my dream to give a TEDx talk could become a reality! After recording an audition tape and applying I was overjoyed to be accepted. Once the celebratory squeals settled, that was when the real work began.

It took months of preparation and an abundance of effort to arrive at a place where I felt ready to stand on the stage to share my big ideas. I knew that every word, pause, and intonation had to be well planned.

In terms of feeling "independent" I can tell you that I felt *very* aware of my solitude on that stage. I felt a blend of vulnerability and nervousness but also confidence and certainty about the message I felt led to deliver. Stepping out, by myself, in that moment pushed me to new levels as a public speaker, professional, and woman. There was nowhere to hide.

There were some serious technical issues with my speaker screen that was supposed to prompt me along, should I have any hiccups during my 18-minutes of remarks. Immediately, I got to the center of the stage and realized it was not as we had rehearsed. I could not rely on the screen to guide me forward. I had to trust in the preparation that had brought me to that moment.

I have watched my TEDx[6] a handful of times since and remain pleased with how it all came together and the big dream that it represents. I chuckle when I can see the flicker of panic in my eyes as the teleprompter took a nosedive. I'm thankful that God gave me a big dream and then walked with me until persistence paid off and I was able to have a spotlight moment on the TEDx stage. Through the experience I grew as a speaker, and I achieved something that was terrifying at times. Vulnerability can be a highly uncomfortable place to be, and I was very vulnerable on that stage!

Soon after my successful TEDx I was asked to emcee a regional event that drew a crowd of 500 business leaders. Again, I stood independently on that stage, guiding the evening's program and engaging with the audience. I love seeing patterns of biblical promise at work in my life—as I was faithful with one thing, God brought more.[7]

Failure to thrive independently can mean your dreams go by the wayside. You can't expect anyone to fight for your dreams the way you will. You can't expect anyone to reach inside you and pull out "what it takes" to stand on your own two feet. It's up to you to stand tall as you fully depend on God to provide

---

6. https://youtu.be/k6sszHnSDsM
7. Luke 16:10

every bit of what you need. When you are able to do something challenging, harder than you thought possible, you'll likely feel the adrenaline rush of independence. That's a feeling I know and love. When a rush from independence washes over you, don't forget to prayerfully turn to the Father and thank Him for being with you each step of the way. He is ever present and someone we can always depend on.

> When a rush from independence washes over you, don't forget to prayerfully turn to the Father and thank Him for being with you each step of the way.

A Rock Wall of Independence

Pursuing a rush of independence often comes with pushing through insecurities or fear. While I don't have a fear of heights, I most certainly have a fear of falling from them. I love gazing out from the top of a mountain down across the landscape below. However, if I take a few steps too close to the edge I start feeling dizzy and overwhelmed.

Can you imagine my panic when my parents suggested we go indoor rock climbing for my older brother's birthday? I was in my late 20's and too prideful to admit I was washed in terror at the idea of this indoor climbing wall. Some people would vocalize their fear and offer to come and hold everyone's stuff while they scaled the wall. However, remember that I wrestle with being stubborn and independent to a fault.

We arrived at the climbing wall, went through the safety discussion, and were turned loose to scurry our way up. To my family, this was no biggie. Everyone was full of giggles, high fives, and eager to establish the best path up. While they were busy getting hyped up for the task before them, I was busy being terrified. I felt my sweaty palms, dry mouth, and huge pit in my stomach. I was afraid.

Then, my stubborn refusal to be conquered by fear took charge and I realized I was not going to be overcome by an indoor rock-climbing wall.

The first run up the wall ended up about 10-feet up. I was encouraged to go up just a little and then "practice falling." Remember, it's not the height I hate, it's the fear of falling. It took multiple attempts at "1, 2, 3, go!" for me to truly let go and kick off the wall—and fall. You would have thought I was base jumping off the empire state building with all the anxiety and build up to that seemingly simple moment. I was so scared to jump, beyond what made sense. I was aware of the ridiculousness of my fear even as I stared at my white knuckled grip on the wall. Down below, my family thought I was trying to be funny or cute. I was so egregiously afraid they thought it was an act. *That's* how ridiculous I was.

Clinging to the side of the fabricated wall I had an epiphany. I realized I was being controlled by my fear. Nobody on the ground could save me from myself. This was an internal issue at work and something I had to push through. I became stubborn in my resolve to show that wall who was boss. That's exactly what I did! I went up and down, up and down, up and down, until I was no longer consumed by fear.

Every time I felt the lump of fear rise from the pit of my stomach, I refused to let it conquer me. I raced as fast as I could to the top, working hard to enjoy the process. No amount of cheering from my family had the power to overcome what I was feeling inside, it was up to me to reach deep and determine how that story would unfold. I had to rely on my own inner strength and the scripture logged in my mind about not living in fear.

Leaving the rock-wall that day felt satisfying. It also felt exhausting if I'm being honest. As much as my body was physically put through the ringer my mind and emotions were even more so. To work for a healthy sense of independence and fight our fears in the process is not easy. But oh, it is worth it!

What is a rock wall opportunity in your life? An experience where you are thrust into the ultimate independence and only you and God can work through the challenges? I'm thinking it may be singing a solo in church, delivering that big presentation yourself, signing up for a 5K for the first time, showing up to a public forum and sharing your perspective. There are so many "rock wall" opportunities for you to flex your independence muscle and grow in the process.

Action Item: Pause to write about a rock wall you are actively trying to climb. What challenges are you up against? Is this an opportunity to grow in independence or maybe a chance to lean into your balcony for support.

There's No "I" in God

I love the idea of you getting up on stage, brave and bold. Or the thought of you pushing yourself physically to accomplish your first 5k. Independence doesn't always manifest itself in conjunction with an outward facing confidence. Sure, it can show up on a spotlighted stage, while a room full of strangers watch with anticipation. However, it can also emerge as you step away in solitude to spend time with no one else except you and God. In the quiet you will learn that even in your most independent moments you are actually not alone; God is always there with you.

I think back to my days on sports teams, from basketball to track, and how an overused but effective mantra says, "There is no 'I' in team." True, there is not. There is also no "I" in God. He is God and you are not. Lean into all His power and majesty to be the author and perfecter. Don't forget that even in the moments that you perceive you are fiercely independent, He is ever present.

God is the perfect paradox of helping you live "self-sufficient" because you are fully dependent on Him. When you live in that way, with daily surrender and a heart oriented to God's strength, yours grows in step.

When we express our need for God to guide us and help us we are able to see His power and might show up for all its brilliance![8] In all my independent moments, from patrolling in my police cruiser to standing on a TEDx stage, I know God was ever present with me. He never leaves us, and He never averts His eyes. Remember, He made us, loves us relentlessly, and delights in us.

I hope that you will grasp that your ability to be independent and well supported are qualities you will find as you draw closer to God. The more aware you are of His goodness and provision, the more confident you will be standing tall in independence. Simultaneously, the surer you are of how deeply He loves you, the more deserving of support you will feel and the more freely you will lean into the love of others. You are worth it and wonderful.

---

8. 2 Corinthians 13:5-9

Brave and Bold Steps Forward

I hope you are ready to step into what it can mean for your life, if you intentionally embrace the reality of being independent and supported!

1. Do you find that you lean more toward independence or being reliant upon others?
2. What is something "independent" you can bravely step out and pursue?
3. What makes you hesitate before asking for help from others? What does God's word have to say in response to those hesitancies?
4. Describe a situation in which you were supported by your community. Detail how it felt and what you learned.
5. Who are your balcony people? Write out a list and detail in which areas of life they support you.

CHAPTER 10

AMBITIOUS AND CONTENT

Have you ever wondered if there is something wrong with you? I have. That is a curious place to find yourself! It can be deeply unsettling.

My most memorable reflection around this question happened in a conversation with one of my favorite mentors, my dad. He's incredibly wise and discerning, while also having a proven track record of success. My dad earned his Ph.D the same year he began raising two children under the age of two and simultaneously started his own business, which grew in the decades to come and became wildly successful. When did the man sleep?

Dad has always been the first to affirm his pride in me and is also the first to ask a well-pointed and thought-provoking question. I appreciate that he loves me enough to speak truth into my life and encourages me to pump the brakes when needed. In one stand-out instance he innocently asked a question, with no ill intent, but it was what sent me reeling and wondering, "Is there something wrong with me?"

I had just finished telling my dad that I was preparing to sell my marketing company after 16 months of accelerated growth. I was eager, giddy, and scared. I remember bracing for his reaction because I knew the news was big and surprising. His question caught me completely off guard and was by far the last reaction I expected. He simply asked, "What will it take for you to be content?"

His question was not rhetorical. I could tell he really expected an answer—eeek!

The question sat heavy between us; it was weighty on my spirit and made me instantly feel insecure and even a little embarrassed.

Dad quickly followed up by saying he was just asking questions and clarified he wasn't trying to take a jab. He could tell from my incredibly awkward pause that it didn't land well. In that moment, I had no answer to give him, but I sure had a lot of thinking to do in the moments, and days, to come.

I wonder if you have also had a moment where a question or feedback made you second guess your dreams? It can come from our mentors, friends, or well-intentioned family members, but when it hits, it's hard! I know his question wasn't meant to make me dive deep into an exploration of my deepest motives, priorities and pursuits, but that is what happened! I hope you will take the moments you are challenged as a prompt to explore and gain new understanding of what is motivating and driving you! Don't let the opportunity pass without maximizing on it.

As I considered what my dad asked, I felt like I had to defend my desire to want more. I panicked that I was selfish, greedy or insatiable. I let a revolving loop of unkind thoughts linger in my head. I ping-ponged between ideas that I was making a horrible mistake, that I'm ungrateful and a flake. I was giving myself a horrible emotional beat down, based on nine words that formed one basic question. When I paused the self-delivered onslaught long enough to let reasonable thoughts cross my mind, I realized how off my thinking was.

Upon reflection, I realized that nothing would make my insatiable desire to grow and evolve feel appeased, satisfied and fulfilled. I love continuously improving and experiencing new challenges within life. I have an ambitious hum within my spirit. At the same time, this hunger isn't mutually exclusive with contentment. I have so much peace and gratitude for all the blessings I'm surrounded by and experience.

My ambition is not driven from a place of discontentment. It's driven from a place of possibilities and wonder of all that God might do in and through me. You can be ambitious and deeply content at the same time. It's a fantastic and powerful paradox.

My ambition is about choosing to own every bit of potential and greatness I was created for. It's an outpouring of God's abundance and the limitless possibilities we have when we submit our lives to Him and obediently listen as He directs our next steps. I'm hungry for impact and am operating from a place of conviction that I have much to give and gain from this world. I can—and you can—be unstoppable if we feed our hunger for more in faith-informed ways.

When you are rooted in the Lord, and allow your life to be defined by Him, you are full of endless and exciting possibilities—abundantly more possibilities in fact![1] Think about the

1. Ephesians 3:20

things you are desiring and dreaming about and consider that God has promised you He can do even better. How is that for incredible!?

Surely you can call to mind an example of when God exceeded your expectations. I'm living that reality in my work for New Hope Girls. This

> Think about the things you are desiring and dreaming about and consider that God has promised you He can do even better. How is that for incredible!?

position has allowed me to wake up every day serving God, advocating for women, and using all my experiences and skills. On top of that, this position has made a way for me to be present for my family and love them well. I never saw it coming! I never knew something this great was even a possibility. But it is. God did immeasurably more for me than I could have ever imagined.

I refuse to believe that in this world we are allotted a certain amount of joy, personal growth and dreams. There are too many tastes, textures, adventures, experiences, and people in this world to ever consider ourselves satisfied. God is also far too creative to keep our life linear, fixed, and lukewarm.

At the same time, I don't find myself sitting in a state of want. I don't walk through my home dreaming of how it can be bigger. I don't browse the internet looking for job opportunities with a bigger salary or stronger benefits package. Sure, I have fun daydreams and will wrestle with envy from time-to-time, but this isn't the hallmark of who I am—because I actively refused to let this define me.

I hope you will not let future possibilities rob you of gratitude for the saturation of blessings you experience daily.

You can live a sweetly satisfied life and simultaneously seek growth—these are not mutually exclusive realities.

Dare to Be Ambitious

I wonder if you may be feeling things swirling in your heart that you are too insecure or afraid to own aloud? Don't be afraid of what you are starting to sense. Be willing to believe that God made you for big, beautiful things and the desires in your heart were put there for a reason. You aren't an accident and the passions you feel are not a coincidence. God is just so good like that!

When you feel those inklings swirling, causing you to wonder what might be next. Pray over them. Be intentional to discern where the desires are from and seek a faith perspective to determine if they are part of the plans and purpose for your life.

One of my favorite qualities of God is just how willing He is to listen.[2] Sometimes I wonder if He sits back and listens intently, all while sipping a heavenly cup of coffee. It puts a smile on my face when I think of Him in all His majesty and glory smiling as we pour our hearts out. He wants to hear from you!

Do you find yourself craving more? I hope you bravely answered YES! Dare to be ambitious, my friend! Like I once did, you may be fighting a really negative voice in your head right now that is telling you wanting more is synonymous with being ungrateful. That's a lie.

You can be flooded with gratitude for all the blessings you have and simultaneously feel deep desires in your heart. Don't try to superficially satisfy the desires you feel, especially when you are prayerful and confident that God is leading the way.

2. Jeremiah 29:12-13

In addition to pursuing your longings washed in prayer, there are practical ways you can begin to explore what might be next. For me, it often means brainstorming, researching, and learning more about the nature of my dream or aspiration. This puts more concrete around the dream.

I also like to visualize the feelings nestled deep within me by creating a vision board. Instead of seeing it stuck inside my head it starts to take a more concrete form as I assign images and key words to the idea. Think of it like an old-fashioned bulletin board with snippets from magazines cut and tacked to the board, all pointing to what you imagine in your head. Another similar concept is a Pinterest board where you grab pins of inspiration to demonstrate your vision for something, maybe Christmas decor, your new home, recipes you love, or fashion. Do the same for your life!

When I was preparing for my major career pivot from owning my business to working in Higher Education, I knew I needed to be intentional about casting a vision for that season of life. It was a major change, a major new job role, and was going to result in a lot of adjustments for our family. I could feel and sense what I wanted this next phase to look like, but I knew that if I didn't feed my hunger for what was next, it wouldn't spontaneously happen for me.

I created a visual layout to depict how I wanted my marriage, home, parenting, lifestyle, faith, and wardrobe to look moving into the new year. When I could see it, my goals had more clarity and visual markers of success.

There are ways that we can supplement our faith pursuits with practical next steps, all while staying rooted in God's truth as our ultimate guidepost.

When you lose sight of your identity in Christ you may allow insecurities and doubts to squash your ambition. You may get in your own way by responding to the dream with a two-word question: "Why me?"

There may be an opening at work and an opportunity for a promotion. You start to consider whether you might be the right person for the job, but then you think—"Why me?" Surely there must be someone more qualified.

You could have a great new idea for how to positively impact your community but don't share it because you wonder: "Who am I to have this great idea? Why me?" You may talk yourself out of sharing your idea because you are certain someone else has the same idea or maybe even a better one.

Maybe you aspire to lead a small group within your church, but when you start to think about it you second guess yourself. You doubt your faith is strong enough or your knowledge of the Bible is sound enough—"why me?"

Self-doubt and insecurities lead you to tell yourself no and to silence your ambition. I encourage you to remember how God has gifted you with a unique set of skills, passions and talents. He has planted passions in your heart that can be used for His good and His purposes. With that in mind, let's turn that two-word question into a much better three-word question!

Why Not You?!

Remember that promotion? Why not you?!

Remember your great idea for how you can positively impact the community? Why not you?!

Remember the desire you had to lead a small group? Why not you?!

When you hold yourself back you are not only getting in your own way, but you are robbing everyone else of the opportunity to experience the wholehearted version of you. Allow yourself to lean into the desires God plants in your heart. Trust that if you abide in Him, He will walk with you.[3] God always provides for us and gives us what we need.

Soul Satisfaction

As much as I love the adrenaline rush of a new idea and the thrill of pursuing that idea. I'm also so abundantly thankful for all that I have and what has been entrusted to me each and every day thus far. Just as my soul seems to stir for more there are a myriad of sweet corners of contentment, where I feel satisfied and full.

I know when I'm most content. It's when I'm sitting on my couch between 5:30–6:30 am, a warm cup of coffee in hand, fuzzy socks on my feet, and a cozy blanket on my lap. I love the beautiful simplicity that those physical things represent, and I adore how they remind me of all that is wonderful and good in my life. My favorite gifts from God.

I have a warm home, a loving family upstairs, the safety to think and dream, a God who loves me and listens to my early-morning prayers, and to top it off—coffee in my cup. So much good is revealed to me as I sit on the couch. I want nothing more than that sweet moment of serenity. It's the picture of contentment.

---

3. John 15:4-11

What really breeds contentment though is not what you see but what is taking place. As I sit on the couch, I use it as time to ground myself in God's word and orient my heart to Him in prayer. When I start my days in this quiet submission to Him, I find that my perspective and satisfaction as the day unfolds is much more solid and rooted in truth. This is how I actively "take captive every thought" as we are instructed to do and ensure my day starts in alignment with the Lord.[4]

It may seem that the image of me sitting cozy on my couch is a juxtaposition to the woman who seems to crave career adventure and the exciting "next thing." Like you, I'm complicated. These complexities make a lot of sense to me, because I'm increasingly sure of who God has made me to be. I'm a dreamer and achiever wrapped in gratitude and satisfaction. What about you, are you content too?

Gratitude and Contentment

If you struggle to feel content—or want to intentionally refine this quality within yourself—I suggest the pursuit of gratitude. Gratitude and contentment are as fantastic together as peanut butter and jelly—or better yet avocado and bacon!

I have learned that there is a correlation between contentment and my ability to actively pursue gratitude in my life. Yes, I think being grateful requires an active pursuit. It's funny though, when I consider how our society personifies gratitude, I see a sweet ole granny in a pastel knit sweater, who slowly reaches into her purse to pull out a caramel flavored hard candy. I'm convinced this is the way the world

---

4. 2 Corinthians 10:5

imagines gratitude. When not a person, gratitude is watercolors and calligraphy script, yielding and passive.

I see gratitude differently. I personify gratitude as an athlete. Specifically, I see her as an Olympic long-distance runner. She laces up her shoes, face like flint, absolutely certain she will run the good race and pursue God's version of truth. He will define who she is and if you try to dissuade her, you better watch out! When she begins to tire and feels her energy waning, she will focus afresh on the blessings that abound and in it, she will find the will to keep pushing. Gratitude is active and energizing! Gratitude is bold colors, a block font, steadfast and resolved!

Think about one of the most celebrated Kings within the Bible, King David. Take a minute to flip through the book of Psalms with an eye for the amount of times David thanks and praises God. It is saturated with gratitude! Go ahead and pause to read Psalm 100 as a starting point. All of those expressions of thanks came from a mighty king—a warrior. So yes, I do see gratitude as an athlete, and I do believe she is fierce.

The pursuit of gratitude is our faith-in-action fight! It's also a stubborn resolve to look past the heartache of our broken world and fix our eyes firmly on our Living Hope. Jesus truly is our author and perfecter.[5]

Sometimes being content almost seems to be frowned upon in our society of go-go-go and more-more-more. As if we should always be planning

> The pursuit of gratitude is our faith-in-action fight! It's also a stubborn resolve to look past the heartache of our broken world and fix our eyes firmly on our Living Hope.

---

5. Hebrews 12:2

the next vacation, next career move, next activity for our kids, or next renovation project. The world says we should always want more. A new pair of shoes, new home decor, new kitchen appliances, new furniture. We should be pushing for a bigger salary, bigger house, bigger vacation. It's as if there is no such thing as enough when it comes to material prosperity.

In contrast to our Olympic athlete of gratitude, the materialistic rat race gets you nowhere but exhausted and begrudged. Pursuing the next best thing really does make me think of a goofy little hamster on a wheel. Racing frantically but headed nowhere incredibly fast! Blind ambition, absent of a grateful heart and commitment to God's ways, is a disastrous hamster wheel of doom.

In God's economy we are urged to remember that where we are prioritizing our time, energy and thought life—there our hearts will be too![6] Understanding and receiving His truth is important and then we can look to practical ways to apply and live in accordance with His will for us.

When we are content with the material possessions we have, we spend less, save more, and can bless others more abundantly. Less stuff keeps things simple, and it allows us to spend money on adventure and experiences rather than items that will gather dust or become obsolete next season.

Contentment extends beyond things we can hold in our hand. I work to be content with who I am today—even if I'm simultaneously excited about who I will be tomorrow. I love the life I've been blessed with, even with all the twists and turns. I do find that from time to time I end up in a disgruntled space where I seem to have blinders

---

6. Matthew 6:19-21

on when it comes to the abundance of blessings that surround me.

Often my lack of contentment relates to timing—I'm relentlessly impatient, it's true! I regularly wonder why God isn't moving faster! I can't understand why I would be asked to wait! In those instances, I kick my own tail back into shape with reminders of how faithful God has been to me across the duration of my life and how His timing is always perfect.[7]

There is always something to be thankful for. Some days it may only be the air in your lungs, but that is still something. Gratitude and thankfulness breed contentment.

Be Still and Know

I wonder if your life is already oversaturated and any attempt to dream feels wildly impossible. Or maybe you feel in survival mode, racing from one thing to the next, and have zero time left for reflection. So many of us live daily lives full of lots and lots of noise that drowns out the profound realizations needed to propel us forward to a life that shines with both ambition and contentment.

The dings and chirps of social media notifications.

Our smart watches reminding us to drink more water.

Our calendar buzzing about our next appointment.

---

7. Ecclesiastes 3:11

A TV on in the background.

Kids crying for a snack.

Bosses reaching out with a quick question.

Music constantly playing, while we go about our daily tasks.

I'm truly concerned that the majority of us have structured our life, technology use, and daily realities in such a way that there is no margin left for quiet. I'm worried you are not getting enough silence in your days.

Quiet can be terrifying to some people and avoided at nearly all costs! Often, we squirm in silence and feel a faux-sense-of-peace when the sensory void is filled with some sort of noise—any noise—that will allow our minds to stay distracted.

While quiet is scary to many people, it's also ironically life-giving to both our wildest dreams and our heartfelt gratitude.

I see dreams as a living thing, and living things need food, water, shelter and also space to exist. Living things aren't meant to be restricted, and if they are, they start to decline in health. They must be protected and nurtured. However, we live in a world that ignores the living and breathing qualities of our dreams and fails to give them conditions to establish roots and bloom to fruition. We must be intentional to fight for these conditions for our dreams to succeed.

For me, the pursuit of margin and quiet is a constant battle but one I'm certain is worth fighting for. I choose to silence my phone and put it out of reach so that I can sit without distractions or interruptions. I escape to my basement office when the daily sounds get to be too much, and I know my mind needs space to soar. I take off for a rhythmic run when I need time in my own head and clarity of thoughts.

Most importantly, in the quiet I'm able to hear God in the most loud and clear ways. He is my ultimate encourager and urges me forward when my dreams feel out of reach or discouraging. Simultaneously, many quiet moments have been spent in a place of conviction because I realize that envy or longing has gone too far, and it's time to humble myself and apologize to God.

Don't be afraid to be alone with your own thoughts. Don't run from the opportunity of nothingness. Most importantly, don't be afraid to quiet yourself before the Lord. "Be still and know" that He is God![8]

One of the beautiful pictures of quieting ourselves before the Lord happens when we meet a highly ambitious woman of the Bible, Martha. In Luke 10:38-42 Jesus Himself stopped by her home, which she shared with her sister Mary. In this story we see that Martha busied herself with a plethora of tasks and perceived needs. In contrast, Mary sat quietly at the feet of Jesus, taking it all in. Martha gets grouchy and calls her sister out (some nerve, right?) asking Jesus to scold Mary for her lack of action. Jesus has such a gracious redirection for Martha: "But the Lord answered her, 'Martha, Martha, you are anxious and troubled about many things, but one thing is necessary.'"[9]

I wonder if at this moment you would be willing to swap your name out for Martha. I'll go first: "Caitlyn, Caitlyn, you are anxious and troubled about many things, but one thing is necessary."

Consider this sisterly encounter as a reminder that God doesn't need your ambition or action to love you. You are simply and sweetly enough. He will invite you

> God doesn't need your ambition or action to love you. You are simply and sweetly enough.

---

8. Psalm 46:10
9. Luke 10:41-42

into His work and guide the desires of your heart, please don't mistake that for needing to "do it all" and "be it all." You are enough for Him. Please sit contently at His feet because that is the one thing necessary.

Your day doesn't have to be punishingly packed with appointments and meetings for it to be worthy. Your family doesn't need a color-coded extracurricular schedule for you to be a good mom or wife. Productivity and noisy days are not accurate ways to measure your impact or importance. They are however a way to distract yourself from the desires of your heart and the blessing of soul satisfaction.

Simplify your schedule. Silence all the sounds. Embrace margin.

Always Changing, Always the Same

It makes me happy that I have so many "dad stories" to tell. Who knew he would be my shining star for this chapter!? Hopefully that means you are realizing what an awesome man he is!

Back before I sold my business (which means back before that semi-awkward conversation about contentment) dad and I went to the coast of Maine together, just us two. It was a weekend trip in November that we dubbed our "CEO Retreat." At that time, we were both leading businesses but in vastly different seasons and circumstances. My dad was finalizing his exit strategy after successfully growing his business for over 35 years. I was in the middle of a growth explosion with my startup of 9 months. Nothing was wrong, in fact because everything was going so right it felt all the more important to step away to pray, reflect, and plan.

That crisp November weekend was one for the books! Dad and I spent a good deal of time together eating fantastic food, hiking, and climbing along the rocky coastline. We balanced that time with solitude. I remember raking the expansive front yard and enjoying the rhythmic manual labor. The instant gratification of piling up leaves was satisfying. I also took off on my bike to explore the coastline by myself. Our retreat was beautifully balanced between alone time and togetherness.

One of the standout aspects of the trip, that still puts a grin on my face today, was how I earned my nickname of Sunset Chaser. Each evening I drove off in pursuit of a new coastal vantage point. I was captivated by the colors as their radiance slowly faded to black. I sat immersed in the beauty as I watched the vibrant artwork in the sky mark the end of one day and the promise of the next. Do you love a stunning sunset as much as me?

The coast of Maine has an eerie and magical quality in late autumn. At this time of year, the tourists have gone home, and the air is still. It was electrifying as I experienced silence and the significance of creation, just me and God present for the nightly sunset shows.

When dad and I were recapping and chuckling about my newfound identity as the Sunset Chaser we marveled at a truth about sunsets. It's obvious and profound, all at once. Each sunset is constantly changing, but always the same.

Each sunset is the opportunity for a new vibrancy of colors, new views, new marks of beauty across the sky. But yet, there is something so peacefully comforting and predictable about a sunset. You can look up the time that the sun will set and with a great deal of accuracy learn the minute the sun will dip below the horizon. It's rhythmic and expected yet surprising and varied, all at once.

Like each sunset, you are also constantly changing but always the same. It's a profound and beautiful truth. You are an opportunity. A possibility for newness, growth, change and development. Yet, at the same time there is something so comforting about the unique qualities and fabric that underpin who you are. There is such a sweet familiarity to who you were created to be. But there is also the air of excitement about how God may invite you to grow and develop.

I encourage you to see yourself as one person with one set of passions, skills, dreams, and talents, but also as ever evolving. Be bravely ambitious for what might be, and boldly content with what is.

Brave and Bold Steps Forward

Are you ready to step into what it can mean for your life, if you intentionally pursue contentment and a hunger for more? Remember, you are worth it and wonderful and that's why exploring this is so important!

1. In what areas do you naturally have a deep sense of contentment?
2. What are your biggest dreams you have been afraid to vocalize?
3. What is one step you can take to actively pursue your God-given potential?
4. Write out 20 (yes, 20!) things you are deeply grateful for. And if you have more than 20, keep going.
5. What is one way you can create more margin to pray over and reflect on your dreams?

CHAPTER 11

ADVENTUROUS AND WISE

The wind was rushing through my hair. I was settled on the back of a motorbike, scooting down the streets of LaVega. The sights and sounds of the busy Dominican Republic sidewalks delighted me. A myriad of colors, textures, smells, and sounds captivated my senses. The roads were unforgivingly marked with potholes, and I was strikingly aware of this reality as we weaved to avoid them. We were part of a flock of motorbikes that seemed to move together in coordinated chaos.

It felt wild. Unruly. Unrestricted. Freeing. A mini adventure nestled within my most recent visit to the DR.

"If only my mom could see me now ..." kept running through my head. Yes, if only!

Maybe it's a good thing she couldn't.

I threw my head back and laughed as I embraced this primary mode of transportation within the impoverished community. Cocolo, my friend driving the motorbike, was cruising along at an incredibly cautious pace, knowing he had a newbie riding on the back. He was probably bored and totally underwhelmed by the pace he was traveling, but he was honoring my wishes to be careful.

I wanted the fun adventure on the back of that motorbike, but I also didn't want it to be too reckless. I wanted to make it to our destination still attached to the motorbike and injury free.

Just as I hoped, we arrived safely, and I had a big smile on my face! That was the first of many experiences on the back of a motorbike in the Dominican Republic. I have grown to love the adventure! And now Cocolo can pick up the speed a bit.

As I have grown and drawn closer to the Lord, I find that my sense for adventure has been unlocked in lockstep. It has been such a curious correlation and unexpected in many ways. I have realized that part of being able to freely embrace adventure is the simultaneous growth in wisdom. Wisdom equips adventure and adventure can produce additional wisdom.

> Part of being able to freely embrace adventure is the simultaneous growth in wisdom. Wisdom equips adventure and adventure can produce additional wisdom.

Entering into the paradox of embracing adventure and wisdom is an exploration of fear, failure, and vibrant living. It invites us to consider where we have built our foundation and how we are pursuing sensibility within our days. It also urges us to consider if we are living life with delight and wonder.

Each of us has a unique tolerance for risk—from outdoor experiences and travel to career and financial decisions. With

God at the helm, we must navigate how to show up fully and authentically as our most adventurous and wise selves.

Embracing adventure while also being wise is something I regularly work on and revisit, as I remain committed to pursuing a brave and bold life rooted in God's truth. I have fought fear in my own life, and I've been afraid of failure. There have been areas of growth I've had to be humble enough to take redirection and correction, in order to live with increased wisdom. It's a process. I'm in-process, and you are in-process!

Are you primarily a risk taker? Or, maybe you are more measured and like living more cautiously? Better yet, do you find yourself willing to grab into life with both hands, all while using faith and truth as your guide? I hope this chapter will be a fun exploration of adventure and wisdom, encouraging you to experience God's abundance in your life.

Over the course of my career journey, I've heard people talk about me (to my face or otherwise) as someone who is bold and takes on a lot of risk. Maybe it's because I was a cop, or an entrepreneur, or because I love riding on motorbikes in the Dominican Republic. But interestingly enough, I don't feel like a risk taker.

Sure, owning my own business was a risky endeavor. But I never really saw myself as a thrill-seeking entrepreneur. I always felt like my risks were measured and I took baby steps towards growth and company development. I do know that when I'm grounded in my faith, I have much less fear, much more wisdom, and enjoy captivating adventures. In many ways, I just consider myself along for the ride, a happy passenger and participant in God's excellent adventure of my life.

Contemplating my career journey, I realize that I do like a certain amount of situational-based adrenaline. I like riding the highs and lows and ultimately coming out on top. With that in mind, I'm also consistently cautious and work to plan for what comes next. I know I'm someone that really likes to balance risk-taking and risk-mitigating.

Let me be clear though. While I love adventure and a good adrenaline rush, I will never, ever, jump out of a plane nor will I ever bungee jump. When I say never, I mean "not for a million dollars" kind of never. There, I said it. And I mean it.

Our Source of Adventure and Rock of Wisdom

As I consider what I mean by "adventure" I realize that word can come to life in so many fantastic and fun ways. At its core, I'm referring to the concept of grabbing onto God's best with enthusiasm and joy. It's a zest for life wrapped in faith!

Career adventures can be new projects, new opportunities or sharing big ideas. You could also embrace adventure by being brave enough to put in for the promotion and seeing where it will take you next.

Family adventures can be going camping for the first time or choosing to take the big road trip. The adventure can also be more monumental, like moving to a new town or becoming foster parents.

Personal adventure can be overcoming hesitancies and trying a new hobby or artistic expression. Pick up the paintbrush! Dare to sing out loud in front of someone else! Explore what it would like to allow yourself the beauty of vulnerability.

Food adventures (which are some of my favorites!) can mean trying new textures, foods, and flavors that you have otherwise never experienced. Instead of going to your usual spot, go to a restaurant you've never visited before. If you are feeling especially daring, you could put options in a hat and blindly pick one out to determine where your culinary quest will take you.

All of these different examples represent ways of stepping into something new or exciting, which also means experiencing more of God's creation and wonder in the process.

One aspect of being able to say yes to adventure is how you are able to intentionally grow in wisdom. I like to think of wisdom as the applied accumulation of common sense or our ability to do life well, with sound judgment. This type of living doesn't just happen by accident.

You can't hope to simply absorb wisdom by osmosis as you float through life. Gray hair and age spots don't mean that your wisdom is magically increasing as those signs of aging appear. You must intentionally seek to grow in good judgment, sensibility, and shrewdness. Open your eyes, reach out your hand, and grasp opportunities for growth.

I'm not sure about you, but I still love to build sandcastles! I love the sensory experience of sweeping sand into piles, patting it down firmly, and using tools to design the castles of my daydreams. It's even more fun when I find little shells and ocean treasures that can decorate and adorn the royal residence. The ultimate highlight is when the kids and I get our hands dirty together and craft a network of tunnels and moats between our castle creations.

Open your eyes, reach out your hand, and grasp opportunities for growth.

The major downside to building a house of sand is that nothing about it is firm—certainly not the construction materials nor the foundation. A house of sand will undoubtedly fall and fail.

This ocean-side reality is why in scripture we are urged to build our lives on a rock—the rock—a firm foundation:

> Everyone then who hears these words of mine and does them will be like a wise man who built his house on the rock. And the rain fell, and the floods came, and the winds blew and beat on that house, but it did not fall, because it had been founded on the rock.[1]

Our wisdom must first be found in our faith and within the intentional pursuit of Jesus. No, this is not some sweet Sunday School answer—Jesus is truly our all in all. As we read in scripture, seeking this type of wisdom is what will help us sustain the storms of life.

Jesus modeled this for us as he grew—He was said to increase in "wisdom and in stature and in favor with God and man."[2] There are three cool components here that we should unpack and consider!

The growth in wisdom that Jesus experienced "increased," which reflects that it was not an instantaneous assignment of judgment and applied common sense. There was a process around wisdom-growth. Additionally, the wisdom He obtained related to both His favor with God and with man—important for us to also consider the relevance and importance of "both."

As women of faith, we ultimately are seeking to please God first in our lives. However, even the scripture acknowledges

---

1. Matthew 7:24-25
2. Luke 2:52

that wisdom also relates to how we interact with other people. While the first aspect of growing in wisdom is directly related to how deeply we know God and the level of intimacy we are experiencing with Him, there is also a component for how we are growing in practical wisdom as temporary citizens of Earth.

We are encouraged to be in this world—but not of the world, which is an acknowledgement that as Christians we are kingdom-bound but currently residing on planet Earth.[3] We need to still live within the reality of our world and make the most of our time here—living lives that reflect the way our faith drives and shapes us. This faith-rooted wisdom should impact the way we spend our money, the career decisions we make, the physical risks we take, and the zest with which we live. As we embody wisdom, we are depicting what it means to live with a rock-solid faith foundation.

Operating with discretion and discernment reflects our understanding of who God is, what He is asking of us, and who He made us to be. People will notice. They will be keenly aware that you manage to walk the line between prudence and fear, adventure and recklessness. They will be so curious about how you are able to live with freedom and fun, while also using sensible judgment along the way. Your faith can be your differentiating factor!

Embrace adventure while also displaying wisdom, because this is a fun way for you to show the impact of your faith on your life.

Embrace adventure while also displaying wisdom, because this is a fun way for you to show the impact of your faith on your life.

3. John 17:15-16

CHAPTER 11

Ridgelines and Failure

Failure is something many people live in crippling fear of. It's the big bad boogeyman that follows them down streets and is hiding under their bed, waiting to spring an attack. Failure is the evil villain that thwarts our big dreams for adventure. I believe many people think failure is always fatal. I'm not convinced of that—except as it relates to jumping out of planes or bungee jumping.

The way I choose to conceptualize failure was shaped by one of my all-time favorite people, my Grampy. Grampy, my maternal grandfather, was an incredible man and community servant. In his retirement, he lived on the coast of Maine and was a fireman, medical emergency responder, school bus driver, recreational lobsterman, and dedicated runner. Grampy ran 80 marathons in his lifetime, to include the Boston Marathon nineteen times. He passed away very young, at the age of 60, only months before he would have completed his 20th Boston Marathon.

Many of the lessons I learned from Grampy were simply the result of watching him live life. His heart for service, love for community, commitment to our family, and dedication to running have helped shape who I am today. Although he passed over twenty years ago, I still carry so much of him with me today.

One lesson I still hold onto is how Grampy taught me to mitigate risk. Funny, I'm not sure he meant to impart such sweeping wisdom, but that's the kind of guy he was. Even in the ordinary, he was wise.

The lesson was delivered as I played along the rocky Maine coastline. Grampy and Nanny lived about ten minutes from the Pemaquid Point Lighthouse, which is the one depicted on the back of the Maine quarter. Pemaquid Point is iconic, lovely, and stately. Perched along rows of rocky ridgelines, the beauty will take your breath away. As you inhale, your lungs will be flooded with the dense and salty sea air.

To this day one of my favorite things to do in Maine is visit the lighthouse and walk along the rocky ridgelines. It's an opportunity to live out my Spiderman dreams as I walk and scramble across the outcroppings. Sometimes I can navigate the rocks on two feet and at other times I need all four-points of contact to hold on and make it safely to the top.

The ocean is rhythmically relentless as it beats against the rocks. I remember having a healthy amount of fear instilled in me by my parents and grandparents as they explained the water was beautiful but unfriendly. The water pummeling the jagged rocks is too aggressive and over-powering. You can hear its power as it churns and breaks against the cliffs, roaring all the while. If I fell in, I would be a goner. There is truly a point of no return at Pemaquid Point Lighthouse.

Here's where Grampy's wisdom comes alongside that rocky reality to provide sage guidance. He instructed that when climbing and exploring we must always leave a rocky ridge-line between ourselves and the ocean. He explained that with a ridgeline between us we always had a place to fall. While we would be hurt if that worst-case-scenario happened, we would not be swept out to sea or battered against the jagged rocks by the waves.

While it was intense advice to receive the grave reality of a misstep made it a necessity! I took his advice to heart because it made a lot of sense, and I knew it would keep me safe. At the same time, I still loved the thrill of scurrying up the rocks, climbing over the edges and carefully pushing the boundaries in a measured way. It didn't instill fear but, rather, wisdom and prudence.

His advice holds true and still makes so much sense, even when I'm not actively scurrying over rocky outcroppings.

Let's create conditions where there is always a ridgeline between us and rock-bottom failure. Failure that leaves bumps, bruises, and stings is okay. Failure that sweeps us out to sea is not. Use wisdom as you set yourself up for safe-failure that is forward-focused and not devastating. In scripture we are reminded that wisdom is more valuable than gold and fools without wisdom will come to ruin.[4]

> Let's create conditions where there is always a ridgeline between us and rock-bottom failure.

A simple example is wearing a helmet. Go ride your bike, feel the wind in your face and the sun on your back, but protect your noggin while you do it. That way if the neighborhood cat runs in front of you while you're cruising along you can wreck (fail) and still have a failsafe (your helmet).

Perhaps more complex is a career decision. If you are starting your own business, consider maintaining an account where you have a financial cushion should there be two or three months in which billings are down or hardship arises. You'll have peace of mind that you can continue forward in your career-adventure because you've put that financial ridgeline in place.

---

4. Proverbs 10:14 and 16:16

To me, these are simple examples of being adventurous and wise at the exact same time. You can step into the paradox in a way that gives life vibrancy without creating conditions for bottoming out and losing it all.

> You can step into the paradox in a way that gives life vibrancy without creating conditions for bottoming out and losing it all.

Risks and Reversible Decisions

If you google the word "Adventure," Google gives results indicating it is "an unusual and exciting, typically hazardous, experience or activity." As we pursue adventure, we open ourselves up to the possibility of hazards—often the hazard of mistakes or uncomfortable consequences.

Adventure and stretching yourself don't have to result in failure, even if you experience results contrary to what you were hoping for. If you are intentional about pursuing safe failure in your life, then you take the edge off of the word and concept. It no longer feels like a boogeyman and instead begins to feel more like a helpful nudge in the right direction. Ultimately, contained failure can lead to learning, growth and development. Best of all, our ability to persevere through hardship and challenges produces character.[5]

Watching my children have small failures is quite exciting to me as a parent. Think about it: If I'm present when they struggle through the frustration of not getting it right, then I can help equip them for future success. I can help them

---

5. Romans 5:3-5

process the struggle and feelings, so they develop resiliency. Life is going to be harsh and hard at times, grit and stick-to-itiveness are qualities we want our children to embody as they grow and mature. The idea that I get to cheer them on and help instill these critical coping skills is an honor and a serious responsibility. Helping my kids fail as they work on elementary school projects or navigate rec-league sports is an enjoyable challenge for me as a parent. They must be able to navigate fear and failure as they pursue a vibrant life.

Helping my kids navigate failure challenges me as well! It forces me to grow because I know they are watching. I'll never forget the day I was telling my husband how defeated I was feeling because of a persistent problem at work. My daughter overheard and said, "Don't worry mommy, you just haven't solved it yet. Don't give up!" Yet. I love that word and all that it represents. It speaks to a solution on the horizon that is coming soon and can be anticipated with certainty.

As you choose to push through the fear of failure, it only makes sense to do so with wisdom. You can be purposeful in choosing situations that push the limits but also include a safety net. When it comes to major life decisions, that can mean knowing your options in advance. Know how to answer the question, "What if this doesn't go well?"

When we established our company, we never intended to have employees or office space. Which means I spazzed a little when I realized early on that I needed additional team members to help my rapidly expanding business. Hiring an employee also meant that I needed office space. I wanted in-person interactions with the team and didn't want them huddled around our kitchen table.

When securing our first office space for Blue Mobius Marketing I chose space in the Virginia Tech Corporate Research Center (VTCRC). Not only did that business complex carry an incredible reputation but they also were exceedingly empathetic to concerns of small business owners. It only required 30 days' notice to terminate my lease. If I experienced business hardships, I knew I would not be stuck with an expensive and seemingly never-ending lease. There was a measured risk in the decision to move into a physical office and out of my kitchen.

Additionally, I had the ability to move into new space within the corporate park at any time. That meant I could expand or shrink, as needed. Which ended up being necessary as we grew rapidly and required a larger space within only three months of moving into the VTCRC.

The CEO of the corporate park helped me navigate risk as a young entrepreneur. He was in essence helping me explore the dichotomy of embracing business adventure while maintaining a wise approach. When we met to tour spaces, I shared honestly about my apprehension to take on overhead costs. I also shared how it felt like the right business move, knowing we wanted an in-person office. He encouraged me to not worry about decisions I could reverse. He helped me see the ridgeline.

This incredible advice really stuck with me and helped me reframe the weight I felt in making decisions as a business owner. Instead of letting myself feel overwhelmed by the enormity of all the decisions I was facing, I found myself noticing how reversible most decisions were. The advice gave me the freedom to simultaneously embrace adventure all while being wise.

You can apply this wisdom in and outside of business context. I love how transferable it is! There are many everyday experiences where you can choose adventure because the decision is reversible. Don't give into the trap to see circumstances as more dire than they are.

Hair will grow back—go for the fun and sassy cut!

Nail polish color can change—be bold next time you are selecting a manicure color! Order something totally different off the menu—don't get the same old thing you always do!

Switch up your vacation destination this coming year—if you don't love it, return to your previous one the following year.

Apply to grad school and take just one class—if it isn't for you, you don't have to continue.

Action Item: How can you release the pressure of making a perfect decision by considering how reversible it is in nature? If an example comes to mind, take out a journal and notepad and write about all the ways you can "undo" the decision, if needed.

Don't Stay in the Car

I wonder if you read my narrative about the gorgeous Maine coast and thought, "I would just stay in the car." Maybe you would put the window down to at least enjoy that salty air. If you did that, you would at least hear the ocean roaring in the distance and you'd simultaneously be so much safer, right? You would undoubtedly avoid the bumps and bruises altogether! No risk of failure. No possibility of pain.

True. You could approach life comfortably from the passenger seat but, wow, you would be missing out. While you would avoid risk you would also avoid fullness and joy. As you experience God's creation—both people and places—your eyes will be opened wider to all that He is and all that He has done. Don't rob yourself of the opportunity to experience that immersive level of wonder and awe.

How can you choose adventure in your own life? Start by recognizing the tough aspects of what you are endeavoring to do and determine if it's worth it. Consider if you are willing to absorb some measure of risk and if you have a safety net—or ridgeline—in place.

If you have been dreaming of a far-off vacation but have been putting it off because it seems outlandish, now is the time to start Googling flights! Start the process and the planning. Make it happen. We are blessed with a big, beautiful world full of possibilities. Go enjoy it with gratitude in your heart.

As you go, expect to grow. We grow as we meet new people who are both dramatically different from us, but also the same in unexpected ways, while undoubtedly also made in the image of God. Our lives become more vibrant as we experience new flavors for the first time. Our worlds are enriched by new cultures and unfamiliar places.

My sister is someone in my life who knows how to choose adventure! Her adventure-loving-spirit shows up in how she travels with her family. She lives in Alaska and early on decided that her kids were going to travel. Even as infants they would hop on a red eye and head out somewhere fantastic and fun.

Those adventures aren't without risks or hardships. Most specifically, the hardship that happens when you have two young kids on extensive airplane flights. I'm pretty sure each flight makes her question her wisdom in signing up for that "fun" and paying so much money to be tortured 31,000 feet in the sky. If they didn't endure the tough parts, they wouldn't get to experience the joy of travel and new places.

You really could just stay in the car. Or just stay home. You could choose to fully avoid the risks of adventure altogether. You absolutely could live this way! However, attempting to insulate yourself from any possibility of hardship is choosing to stop living while you are still breathing. Living overly cautiously and wrapped in fear is choosing to live diluted and bland. It's also a reflection of a faith struggle related to trusting that God really is in control of all our todays and all our tomorrows. God really does have the whole world in His hands.[6]

> Attempting to insulate yourself from any possibility of hardship is choosing to stop living while you are still breathing.

There is so much unknown as we journey through life, but what we do know, and must cling to, is that God is in control. That is what gives us the freedom to embrace adventures of all types.

As I embraced the adventure of owning a business, I got to help provide jobs for some of the coolest people I've ever met! I pushed myself professionally and learned so much along the way—lessons I carried into the next career adventure. My

---

6. Psalm 95:3-6

husband and I also got to experience the fun of being business partners and growing a company together. It refined us and brought us together in increased unity. Had I said no, when God presented me with this opportunity, I would have never experienced those blessings.

Every time I embrace the adventure of traveling to the Dominican Republic I grow as a traveler, woman of faith, and global citizen. I have favorite food I can only get while in the country that I crave while I'm back stateside—like seafood mofongo! I've learned what it's like to be in a place where I don't speak the primary language. It has taught me so much about how many different ways people can live, love, and worship God. My perspective has been blown out to a wide-angle view because I'm willing to say yes.

I would love for you to live bravely and boldly with an adventurous spirit. I'm certain that in doing so your life will grow in dimension and depth. I want you to taste and see the goodness of God, as you trust Him to accompany you on all of life's many adventures.

Fear Not

Excellent adventures are the kind of stories that people want to hear. They are the ones that captivate attention and cause folks to lean in, elbows on their knees, eyes wide, minds chasing each word to see where it will go next. Adventures are the experiences that wake us up and remind us we are alive as we explore and experience something new or strikingly different. I wonder if you are embracing enough adventure in your life or if you have gotten too comfortable playing it safe?

Living a life marked by adventure can be incredibly difficult when fear creeps its way into your heart and mind. It's a poison that comes to kill and steal your opportunity to embrace joy.

Fear often likes to masquerade as wisdom, logic or reason. It invites us to overthink situations, over emphasize our cognitive processes, and forget about God's sovereignty. I'm not immune to these thought-life struggles and must fight the urge to let wisdom morph into fear. I hope you'll join me in the fight back against fear!

It's important we invite others into our struggles and use it as a way to affirm "it's not just you—I've been there too!" If you'll indulge me, I'd like to walk you through an active fear-struggle and how I'm fighting back.

As I joined the rest of the world in navigating the Covid Global Health Pandemic I found myself struggling with fear, for the first time in a long time. It's strange because I really have been a generally fearless person my entire life. But the pandemic, and saturation of tragedy and sadness in the media, creeped into my confident stronghold and started to create fissures. The weirdest thing of all is how it caused me to develop a fear of flying.

All I can figure is that the daily conversations around death, dying, hardship and mortality caused a kink in my otherwise fearless armor. I no longer let faith and truth guide my thought life. Instead, I let my emotions take control. It feels yucky to admit that, but at its core, that is what was going on.

For the first 33 or so years I was not afraid of flying. And then one day, it all changed. I felt myself fighting a panic attack as I took a seat on a small plane from Charlotte to Roanoke. Every dip and altitude change made me convinced the plane was failing and they just hadn't told us yet. I was certain we were going down and that the flight attendants knew it but were staying calm, so we'd all go down peacefully. I was a mess! It defied logic!

As I'm sure you can surmise, the flight landed safely. We were totally fine. Nothing was wrong. I made it all up in my head. Yet, that experience allowed the fear to take root.

Being afraid of flying is problematic if you are someone who loves traveling—which I am. It's also a challenge when you work for an international non-profit that requires 3 flights each way. Which I do.

Since flying isn't a daily or monthly experience, I was able to ignore the fear for a while. But there came a day where I knew I wanted to decline a trip not because of my schedule but because I was too afraid to fly. I hated that moment when I realized the real reason I didn't want to travel: fear.

We all have our fears. Maybe flying is no big deal for you, but there are other situations that cause you terror and anxiety. Sometimes I worry that we indulge and nurture our fears, wearing them as a self-deprecating badge of honor. You can acknowledge the fear, own it, and choose to not give it another inch within your life.

The Bible is so very clear that we are NOT called to live a fear filled life.[7] I claimed this reality as a police officer and held to it with stubborn resolve when facing melanoma, but yet I was choosing fear as it relates to flying. I felt really convicted about my role in allowing the fear to take root and multiply in my heart. I know that there are situations in which our bodies have imbalances that lead to emotional problems, but this was not what was happening with me, and I knew it. It was not a brain chemistry issue—it was a faith issue.

---

7. Joshua 1:9

Even though I wanted to decline the trip and stay home to wallow in my fear, I felt certain God was asking me to go. I feel a call on my life as it relates to New Hope Girls and my answer is yes. So, with anxiety abounding, I booked the trip. A total of 6 flights to get there and back.

Over the duration of those 6 flights to and from the Dominican Republic I decided to actively fight my fear. It wasn't easy or comfortable. But with my Bible in hand, I forced myself to read scripture as we sailed through the skies. With determination, I was committed to controlling my thought life and only thinking of "things that are above, not on things that are on earth."[8] I will not tell you that it was a perfect process, or I had a miraculous moment that cured me of my fear. However, I did find myself improving and gradually trusting God more and more with my life and my emotions.

On the way home, I not only read my Bible, but I implemented a different way to fight back. I started thanking God for the fear. As I write these words to you, I realize how nonsensical it sounds. It sounds disingenuous and like I'm trying to use some "holier than thou" Christian-judo-mind-trick. I promise you, I did it because I felt like I had nothing to lose as I tried to armor up and fight back. I prayed prayers of gratitude for my fear out of desperation to make it go away.

My prayers went something like this:

Dear God. I'm sitting on a plane right now, super afraid. I actually hate this. No part of me likes this. It doesn't feel natural—you didn't give us wings so why am I in the sky? Did you really mean for us to fly? I don't think you did. But you know what

---

8. Colossians 3:2

God... now that I think about it, this is a way to answer your command to 'go to the Nations' and that's pretty great. Back in the day I wouldn't have had this opportunity—or would have traveled for weeks on a boat to get to the DR—so this is more efficient. But I really don't like how this feels. But at the same time, I do love how it feels to be in-country with the women and girls of New Hope Girls, wow I love them. So, thanks for making a way. And for the resources to pay for a plane ride— thanks for that too. And now that I think about it, you remind us how you take care of birds—and birds fly. So, if you take care of the birds, and give them flight, will you do the same for us? Hold this plane in your hand. Hold me in your hand. What a privilege it is to align with your work and to fight for your daughters. God, I really am thankful! Please keep me calm and relaxed as we continue flying, I know these feelings of peace can only come from you. I want to feel your power show up because I'm so very aware of how weak and fearful I am. I know you are big. I know you are bigger than my fear. God, you amaze me!

It was a stream of consciousness conversation with God that He used to reframe and refresh my perspective. If it seems like a rambling prayer, it was. Because it was a completely honest prayer. I wanted to release the fear but wasn't totally sure how to do that. I prayed and He shaped what came next. Truly, I experienced the scriptural truth that the Holy Spirit helps us pray when we don't know what to pray for.[9]

Isn't it amazing that prayer and gratitude were my secret weapons to fear?

I hope that you will consider a stream-of-consciousness prayer session in which you find a way to express gratitude. Don't let

---

9. Romans 8:26-27

yourself be overcome by fear. Offer up honest and raw prayers and trust that God is big enough to handle them and to help you.

> **Action Item:** Pause to consider a fear you are actively fighting. How can you pray about the fear with a framing of gratitude? Spend time doing exactly that. Be expectant for how God will allow you to see the fear differently as a result of your honest prayer.

Remember, when we experience a calling or clear direction on what God expects from us, there's not a footnote to the calling that indicates a loophole of "unless you are afraid." It's the exact opposite! The Bible is beautifully saturated with commands to live without worry and fear—fear and faith are not meant to coexist. God cares about what weighs us down and wants to set us free. Cast your anxieties on Him so that He can help you live worry-free and fully dependent on Him.[10]

Our ability to embrace a bold and brave life, laced with adventure and wisdom, is often in direct correlation to the importance of faith within our lives. Whether in the sky, on a boat, working in your own backyard, God is for you. You can't let the circumstances you are in, even when they are 31,000 feet in the sky, allow you to waiver in your ability to trust in His sovereignty. He's got this! He's got you!

Go Live Your Adventure

I hope you are feeling your heart race with excited anticipation as you consider the dream you've been silencing for far

---

10. 1 Peter 5:7

too long. Whether the dream is a vacation, writing a book, putting in for the promotion, starting your own business or starting a family. You know what you need to do! Approach the dream in prayer and submission to God with direct requests for His wisdom about your next steps. Don't stuff the dream down any longer, stop fleeing from adventure.

If you are already an adventure-connoisseur I hope you will pause for a self-assessment about

> **Don't stuff the dream down any longer, stop fleeing from adventure.**

how you are intentionally seeking wisdom as you go.

Be eager for growth in your ability to live in full color, with sound judgment that allows you to experience God's best in your life.

Brave and Bold Steps Forward

Are you ready to step into what it means to intentionally embrace being adventurous and wise? Have fun exploring the questions below as a way of getting started!

1. Do you find yourself living more of an adventurous life or a life marked by wisdom?
2. What is one fear you are actively fighting? Write out an honest prayer sharing your fear with God. Figure out how you can find gratitude nestled within your fear.
3. What is an adventure you are craving but have hesitated to pursue? Spend time reflecting on the fear or circumstances that are holding you back.
4. How can you grow in wisdom and understanding within an important area of your life?
5. How can you reframe failure and identify "reversible decisions" within challenges you are currently facing?

CHAPTER 12

YOU ARE WORTH IT AND WONDERFUL

Are we really here? Have we really reached the final chapter of this journey together?

We are in fact "here" and this really is the final chapter of this book. Admittedly, I'm a little bummed about that. It has been my joy to walk with you along this colorful exploration wrapped in faith.

As we wrap up, I want to leave you with a few final thoughts, some unifying ideas that pull together everything we have explored and experienced throughout the chapters of this book.

Seasons Change

Because of your unique and continually changing life cir-cumstances, this book, and especially certain chapters of this book, may impact you differently than others. Additionally, the things that spoke to you today may resonate differently in six months or even five years from now. After all, the seasons we are living in provide important context as we seek to live brave and bold lives.

My husband and I are raising our family in southwest Virginia and in this beautiful part of the country we get to experience four true seasons.

Wow, there is nothing quite like the first snow and the quiet hush that comes with the beautiful blanket of white, laid over the Blue Ridge Mountains. Living within the rolling hills and beautiful mountains ensures we have endless options to choose from when we are ready to go sleigh riding.

Then, we get to welcome spring! Beautiful greens return to the mountains and the intoxicatingly fresh air lingers, starting dense and heavy in the mornings. I love walking our kids to the bus in the morning and drawing a deep breath down into my lungs. A gratitude breath because I'm certain I'm breathing in the goodness of God. As we drive in our community, we see the baby farm animals taking their first tentative steps and hear the birds performing symphonies as they sense the welcoming warmth has come to stay.

Those sweetly mild temperatures soon give way to pool weather—summer! It gets hot and with it comes the fun of travel and trips to east coast beaches. We also get to do cannonballs in our local pool, visiting with our friends while we cool off. At night, we sit on our front porch with ice cream cones in hands, talking about everything and nothing.

Then, the heat gives way to early indicators that change is coming. The return to school is a clue that more change is on the way. Soon, the mountains erupt in a myriad of colors—some fiery and fierce, others muted and muddy. Fall is my favorite season, cozy and with crisp temperatures and earthy smells I just can't get enough of! The leaves on the ground. Pumpkin flavored everything. Soups simmering on the stove.

There is something I love about every season—a reason to be thankful when the change comes about. I love how nature looks and feels different as the calendar changes. While there is a cyclical nature and rhythm to the way seasons change, we can also be certain no two seasons will ever be exactly the same.

Our daughter was born in March and the days leading up to her birth I sat out on our back deck in my T-shirt and maternity shorts. Her first birthday was so snowy that some of our favorite relatives couldn't make the drive in to celebrate. The same day on the calendar but a vastly different season-experience.

Life also has a way of cycling through seasons. High school years. The college days. Single living. Newlyweds. Newborn living. Establishing a career. Raising a young family. Parenting teenagers. Empty nesters. Retirees. These all represent distinct seasons and stages of life. When we leave one season, we are never able to fully come back to it, which doesn't have to be depressing and sad! Rather, it's a prompt and a reminder to let the best of each season wash over us.

I love my present season! Our kids are still young enough to be silly, imaginative, and super sweet but are also able to take care of themselves in many ways. They want us around and love family game nights. I'm also very present in their lives because my work with New Hope Girls allows me to focus on them before and after school. I'm fully aware that this season is precious and a gift from above. I also know it won't last forever (*sigh*).

While it pains me to write this, I know that my kids can't stay this way forever. Growth and maturity are necessary as they transition from being young kids to teens and from teens to adults. Even though it makes my momma heart achy to imagine the day they no longer wake me when they have nightmares, I know entering into a new season and watching them grow will be so beautiful.

There is also the reality that my current season is heavily focused on faith, family, and work. It means that little space is left for friends at the end of the day. I own and accept that in this season my family relationships are primary and supported by specific and key friendships. I'm not the girl you'll see traveling for a ladies weekend trip or routinely heading out for dinner with a big group of friends. You will find me at home having dance parties with my kids or heading over to my mom's house for dinner with my parents and my brother's family. I'm okay with that, I recognize it's a reflection of the season I'm in right now.

In stark contrast, my parents are both in retirement and living their best life as empty nesters. They are traveling and away from our home base more often than they are here. It has been so fun to watch them celebrate life together as they bop around from the National Parks to the Dominican Republic, from Alaska to Florida and from the coast of Maine out to California. They are on the go! The shadow side to their exciting reality is that at times they feel like they are out of step with the rest of the world, which is still largely functioning on a Monday through Friday, 8:00 to 5:00 type of schedule.

For each of us, our season will look different and bring with it unique circumstances to navigate. Our seasons will create conditions for success and will present limitations for what we are able to do. At present, I'm not able to travel the world and take a two-week hiatus from life as I know it—but my parents are. One day our nest will be empty and maybe then we will travel around the world and live as wanderers for an extended period of time—but not today.

As you consider how you can grab onto every bit of who God made you to be, release yourself of the pressure to figure it all out today. Recognize that you serve a God who celebrates seasons and recognizes the reality of change in our lives.

> As you consider how you can grab onto every bit of who God made you to be, release yourself of the pressure to figure it all out today.

Don't be discouraged or fearful, change is part of the human experience and a way that God keeps us fully depending on Him. It's also okay to recognize the parts of your season that feel hard, or you hope will change some day. It's not a biblical promise that our lives will be perfectly wonderful from beginning to end. The opposite is true! We are encouraged to know that things will be hard, and we will have to seek perseverance in the Lord, as we go through different seasons and experience change.

Ecclesiastes 3:1–8 (NIV) not only affirms that God has incorporated seasons into our lives but also reminds us of how the seasons we experience can be full of paradox and contrast.

There is a time for everything,
   and a season for every activity under the heavens:

   a time to be born and a time to die,
   a time to plant and a time to uproot,
   a time to kill and a time to heal,
   a time to tear down and a time to build,
   a time to weep and a time to laugh,
   a time to mourn and a time to dance,
   a time to scatter stones and a time to gather them,
   a time to embrace and a time to refrain from
      embracing,
   a time to search and a time to give up,
   a time to keep and a time to throw away,
   a time to tear and a time to mend,
   a time to be silent and a time to speak,
   a time to love and a time to hate,
   a time for war and a time for peace.

Take time to breathe in the goodness of God as you look around your home, work, and community to consider the special aspects of this season that will surely change some day. Each day is one step toward a lifelong journey of whole-hearted living rooted in faith. The seasons will change as you learn to better love yourself for who God created you to be.

As we work to bravely and boldly pursue a life that over-flows with beauty and purpose, to fully own all we have been created to be, we must also recognize that we don't have to own it all today or in this present season. We are a work in progress, and we will constantly have to recalibrate and adjust, as our seasons change. There is freedom in recognizing that we have the ability to ebb and flow as we journey. Trust that your gracious, powerful, and perfect Father will complete every bit of the work He began in you.

He is in the Daily

Maybe you are reflecting on all that you have read and are skeptical because it all sounds a little too good to be true. You may wonder about the next steps and how to live out the reality that you are worth it and wonderful. Don't be overwhelmed—it's in "the daily" that you can find the answers.

> You may wonder about the next steps and how to grab hold of truth to live out the reality that you are worth it and wonderful. Don't be overwhelmed—it's in "the daily" that you can find the answers.

Within the pages of scripture, God is so clear in His request of us. He wants our daily devotion. At no point does God ask us to figure it out for the next week, the next quarter, or the next year. It's in the daily that He shows up to look us in our eyes, love us fiercely, and guide us through our days.

I love the dailyness of our relationship with him. When I think of the people I love the most, they are the ones I'm in "the daily" with. I call my mom daily, after the kids go to school. I sit and visit with my kids daily, around the breakfast table, after they get off the bus, and before bed. I connect with my husband daily, before work, later in the evening. My sister-in-law and I text daily to share life updates and the nuances of our experiences. Point being: The ones I love are also the ones I connect with on a daily basis. I imagine the same is true for you.

Isn't it special that God has a daily affection for you?! You are not a distant cousin, once removed. You aren't a long-lost friend with decades of time and space between you. You have a standing request for a daily connection to the God of the Universe.[1] When this daily practice becomes a regular rhythm in your life, you are inviting abundance into your life.

He Will Provide

As you process all the ideas and things that we have discussed it's my hope that you will lean into God to be The Provider of what you so desperately seek and your heart's desires. I hope that you will recognize your role and the actions you can take, while also allowing Him the time and space to show up as your almighty and sovereign God.

One of my all-time favorite Bible stories is found nestled in Genesis 22. This is when we get an up-close look at how Abraham balanced taking action in his own life while steadfastly trusting that God was the ultimate provider of everything he needs.

In this story, we are invited into a journey between Abraham, his son Isaac, and God. It begins with the Lord giving a very clear and heartbreaking command to Abraham. God said, "Take your son, your only son Isaac, whom you love, and go to the land of Moriah, and offer him there as a burnt offering on one of the mountains of which I shall

---

1. Lamentations 3:22–23

tell you."[2] God literally asked Abraham to kill his son as an offering.

I cannot imagine the anguish Abraham endured as he walked in faithfulness and did what was asked of him. He obeyed with a faith that was greater than his fear and grief.

For more than three days Abraham journeyed with his son to the place the Lord instructed him to go. Along the way, Isaac asked where the sacrifice was and Abraham simply answered, "God will provide for Himself the lamb for a burnt offering, my son."[3] What amazing confidence to display in the face of a looming tragedy!

With his own two hands, Abraham built the altar that he fully believed he would soon use to sacrifice his son. Abraham was so confident in God's goodness, sovereignty, and provision that He was willing to act in faith, even in those unthinkable circumstances.

But moments before Abraham could follow through in faith, an angel halted Abraham as he readied the knife.

"And Abraham lifted up his eyes and looked, and behold, behind him was a ram, caught in a thicket by his horns. And Abraham went and took the ram and offered it up as a burnt offering instead of his son. So Abraham called the name of that place, 'The Lord will provide' as it is said to this day, 'On the mountain of the Lord it will be provided.'"[4]

God delivered when all seemed impossible and lost. God provided a ram.

---

2. Genesis 22:2
3. Genesis 22:8
4. Genesis 22:13-14

Abraham moved faithfully, driven to do the work at hand, while also patiently waiting on the Lord to provide. It's beautiful, encouraging, convicting, and humbling to see the faith of Abraham.

I hope we can all move forward with the faith of Abraham. Certain, even in the direst of circumstances, that what we need will be provided. Steadfast in our faith and willing to go on the journey the Lord is asking of us.

> **Action Item:** Are you praying for a ram right now? Go read through Genesis 22 and consider what faithful footsteps you can take, as you trust is God's provision.

Between You and God

As you take faithful steps forward it's possible that others will not understand what you are up to and why. They may question all that you are taking on or how your brave and bold pursuits make sense. Don't forget, there was a whole community of people who thought Noah was a truly weird neighbor. God's ways are not always our ways—or the ways that our friends and family might suggest.

One subtle critique—and dig—that I have received over the course of my life is, "Don't you think you are doing too much?" It's a nod to the notion that I'm trying to do it all and be it all. There is no way for another person to know the answer to this question without being able to read my mind and search my heart.

The amount on my plate and the internal growth work I'm taking on needs to be guided by God primarily. Secondarily, those closest to me, like my husband or balcony people, can be an additional source of accountability.

There are times that the honest answer is "yes," and I have taken on more than my plate can hold. There are other times that the honest answer is "no" and I'm operating at an optimal place and enjoying the excitement of growth, impact, and fun! My husband is the best person to help keep me balanced and grounded. He loves me deeply, wants the best for me, and will speak up when he thinks the work and commitments on my plate have gotten too much. I'm thankful I can trust him to love me in this way!

Here's a great and recent example. I'm in the process of finishing my master's degree, one class at a time. I signed up for a Summer I and a Summer II class to try to expedite my degree completion, because at 1 class a semester it was moving painfully slow. Well, wouldn't you know that the publishing contract for this book came about mid-semester for Summer I. Did I all of a sudden feel like I was doing too much? Yes, indeed I did! However, tuition was paid, and I was stuck in Summer I.

Summer II was a different story. I knew if I tried to take that class and finish my manuscript—on top of vacation, mothering, New Hope Girls, etc.—I would implode. I ran this all by my husband and he was emphatic I needed to drop the second class and protect my sanity and time. That is what it looks like to "do it all and be it all" with boundaries, margin, and self-preservation in mind.

Don't you dare feel guilt over aspiring for a lot and feeling like God has placed a big call on your life. Remember one of the first scripture verses we visited together—"Thank you for making me so wonderfully complex! Your workmanship is marvelous—how well I know it."[5] God made you capable of so much, especially when your daily walk is arm and arm with Him.

> Don't you dare feel guilt over aspiring for a lot and feeling like God has placed a big call on your life.

In Our Waiting, He is Working

Like Abraham, I'm certain that God will provide for you, refine you, guide you and lead you. My prayer for you is that you can be patient for His perfect timing.

It's ironic that I'm telling you this because I'm admittedly the most impatient person I know. I'm worse than a kid waiting in line for the Slinky Dog Roller Coaster at Disney World. I'm terrible! But God, in His gracious refining power, is working on my heart and helping me calm down, chill out, and embrace patience.

It was while I was on a run that I became aware of the power of patience. I was in the zone and mentally relaxed. Worship music was playing against the sounds of my rhythmic breathing. All of a sudden, a song I had heard countless times hit me in a new and profound way. It was the song "Wait on You" by Elevation Worship and Maverick City Music. This song includes scripture from Isaiah 40:31.

> but they who wait for the Lord shall renew their strength;
>   they shall mount up with wings like eagles;
> they shall run and not be weary;
>   they shall walk and not faint.

---

5. Psalm 139:14 (NLT)

My eyes were opened to the fact that while we wait on God, He prepares us. He gets us ready with the energy that we need and equips us for all that lies ahead. Waiting is actually an amazing gift from above. Instead of seeing it as an inconvenience we can look at it as an opportunity for rest and readiness.

> Waiting is actually an amazing gift from above. Instead of seeing it as an inconvenience we can look at it as an opportunity for rest and readiness.

While we wait, He works. The day that truth washed over me was a powerful day, indeed. I realized that maybe the reason I'm tired so often is because I fail to sit back, relax, and let God be the awesome God that He is. There's a thought for you!

Before you act, wait.

Before you feel compelled to do, wait.

Before you take matters into your own hands, wait.

Wait on the Lord and see how He shows up to renew your strength! The timing with God is always right.

He Is Calling Your Name

My husband was at work and would be stuck there until the wee hours of the morning. I was home with both kids, who at the time were 7 and 9. We just had the most enjoyable night with my parents! They joined us for a culinary experience created by none other than my kids! The kids came up with a restaurant concept, "The Den." We crafted a menu and experience that was both fantastically imaginative and well executed. All the menu items and decor were themed around woodland creatures—specifically foxes. We laughed, ate, and enjoyed—including a spontaneous dance party. Our night was a quintessential evening of family, fun, childhood joy, and delight. The only thing missing that night was my husband.

My parents headed home, and I prepared the kiddos for bed. My heart was full as we moved through our normal bedtime routine of brushing teeth, getting comfy in jammies, and reading books together.

Earlier that morning my son had mentioned a scratchy throat, but I assumed allergies. He mentioned it in passing when he got up for the day but said nothing else the rest of the day—so I forgot about it. No other symptoms showed up, he played fine, and ate fine all day. When I put him to bed, all was right in our world.

I got them both cozy, under the covers, and surrounded by their favorite stuffy friends. I then crossed the hall into our room and began watching my Netflix show du jour. Per usual, I dozed off while watching TV, but at 10:15 something caused me to stir. In my bleary-eyed and half-asleep state my attention was turned toward my son's room. As I threw the covers back and began moving in his direction I heard a terrifying sound—almost a cough but not quite.

I rushed into his room and saw him sitting up in bed, wide-eyed and gasping for air. He was trying to talk but couldn't. Each word required its own breath. I grabbed my phone and called my husband long enough to let him know I was calling 911 (because...he is a first responder and I knew he'd hear the call go out over the scanner and yes, I know, 911 should have been my first dial, but it wasn't ...).

I picked up my son and headed to the bathroom to turn on the hot water and make steam, in an attempt to help his airway open up. One gasping breath at a time my son was saying over and over, "I'm. Going. To. Die." You may think that being a former cop would have helped me keep my cool—but it didn't. To be clear, I was panicked. I was barely coping, still moving through the situation, but inside I was crumbling and crashing fast.

The 911 dispatcher immediately began getting basic information and triaging the situation. She told me help was on the way. But in all the things she was saying, I couldn't stay with her. She became fuzzy background noise while I became consumed with the crisis in my hands, my son struggling to breath. It was a surreal sensory experience where her words hung in a different reality, far off in the distance and disconnected from me. I kept forgetting I was on the phone, overcome by panic.

At this point my daughter had woken up. She was jolted into fear by all the commotion she heard right near her bedroom door. I was doing my best to manage the emotions of all 3 of us, all while keeping tabs on my son's status, and imploring God to see our plight and intervene.

I was drowning in an anxiety spiral of panic, and then I heard my name.

"Caitlyn."

"Caitlyn. You are doing so good. You are doing amazing."

I heard my name. And I listened.

I still cry every time I remember this story and tell this story. I'm crying now. The dispatcher brought me back, up and out of the anxiety spiral. She said my name.

I didn't feel as lost in the darkness of our situation anymore. She called me out of myself. I was then able to focus more, counting my son's breaths for her, receiving reassurance that although his breathing was labored the rate was still normal.

She did it more than once. I would get consumed by the chaos and fear and then I would hear my name.

"Caitlyn, they are almost there."

"Caitlyn, can you keep counting his breaths for me?"

The rescue squad arrived, transported my son to the hospital, and he immediately received incredible care. My husband was waiting on us at the hospital and I instantly felt relief to have him by our side.

The team that showed up that night was handpicked by God, there is simply no other possibility. They were swift and sure with the care they offered while still being empathetic and kind to our family. After being briefly admitted into the hospital, our sweet, silly, enthusiastic little guy was released and returned home, healthy.

That situation is still hard to talk about and remember. It's surely one of the scariest nights I've had as a parent—maybe the scariest. But as I look back on that night, I remember that 911 dispatcher being "my person" when I needed someone so desperately. I remember her bringing calm to my chaos. Most profoundly, I remember and realize that when she called my name, I heard her and responded.

There is a beautiful biblical parallel here. Throughout the pages of scripture, we see the power of a name time and time again. There are all sorts of "biblical greats" who had a name custom picked by the Lord as a representation of who they are and whose they are. Abram became Abraham after making a covenant with the Lord.[6] Saul became Paul after he met Jesus on the road to Damascus and went from persecuting Christians to becoming a disciple of Jesus.[7]

I wonder if you have taken time to consider that God our Father and creator knows you by name. You are worth it and wonderful because the God our Universe, who is expansive, powerful, and vast has chosen to be intimately aware of who you are.

> I wonder if you have taken time to consider that God our Father and creator knows you by name.

When He speaks your name, allow it to beckon you into a place of light and hope. Every bit of being brave and bold is found rooted in who God says you are and who He has made you to be. That is when you will find your cup overflowing, the desires of your heart met, and you'll experience peace that surpasses all understanding.

This isn't some superstitious pursuit or a cosmic "if then" approach to life—"if I pursue God, then everything will be great." Rather, it's allowing Him to enter into all corners of your life, all the paradoxes that don't make sense, all the messy places that feel too complicated, your pain, the heartache, and confusion. It's submitting the best parts of yourself to Him, too! Hand over your dreams, aspirations, and success and joys in loving submission to God. He is simply waiting for your invitation to come in, shine light, and set you free. THAT is what it's all about to recognize we are worth it and wonderful.

He is calling your name—so what is your answer?

---

6. Genesis 17:5
7. Acts 9:1-19

Now Go Be Brave and Bold!

The work you have done as you read through these pages matters. The work you continue to do as you process and reflect matters even more. Remember, nothing of significance is easy or comes quickly. This type of work can challenge deep rooted beliefs—some of which you may realize are lies that took root a long time ago and have grown gnarly and complex over the years. It will likely take wrestling with thorny falsehoods and exploring places that cause you discomfort to push through to new levels of understanding and to continue doing so moving forward. I'm sitting here smiling as I think about you prioritizing this work and persevering in the days to come!

When this book began, I was worried about you, and I didn't hide the fact. Now, I've moved away from worry into a place of hope.

My hope is that our time together has resulted in clarity, insights and inspiration that will encourage you toward faith-shaped living each and every day. As your identity and purpose become rooted in who God says you are, I'm trusting that all areas of your life will start to transform with vibrancy. I believe this for you and invite you to believe it too!

Above all, I sincerely hope that you bravely and boldly embrace the reality that you are worth it and wonderful.

Brave and Bold Steps Forward

Here we are! You did it—we did it! Please remember just how wonderful you are—because God says you are.

As you wrap up this final page, I hope you'll spend time in one last session of reflection and prayer.

1. How would you describe your current season? What about it is sweet—what are the challenges?
2. Reflect on how "daily" your relationship is with God. How can you take steps toward greater connection with Him?
3. What is an area that you are struggling to embrace patience? Pray over this specific situation and God's ability to renew and prepare you, while you wait.
4. What is one practical takeaway from this book that you will implement in your life moving forward?
5. Consider who you can share this book with. Who is someone in your life that needs to hear the message that she's worth it and wonderful?